Choctaw Language and Culture

Choctaw Language and Culture

Chahta Anumpa, Volume 2

Marcia Haag
Henry Willis

University of Oklahoma Press : Norman

Also by Marcia Haag and Henry Willis

Choctaw Language and Culture: Chahta Anumpa (Norman, 2001)

Library of Congress Cataloging-in-Publication Data

Haag, Marcia, 1951–
    Choctaw language and culture : Chahta Anumpa / by Marcia Haag and
    Henry Willis.
        p. cm.
    Includes bibliographical references and index.
    ISBN 978-0-8061-3855-8 (paper)
    1. Choctaw language—Grammar. 2. Choctaw Indians. I. Willis, Henry,
    1929– II. Title.

PM872.H332001
497'.3—dc21

                                                                00–053277

This book is dedicated to the memory of
Malvina Lavina Tubby Willis
and Adam Hugh Willis

Contents

Illustrations

Preface

We are pleased to finally bring forth the second volume of our Choctaw grammar. This book is both a continuation of *Choctaw Language and Culture: Chahta Anumpa* and at the same time something quite different. While the previous volume focused on contributions concerning Choctaw history and culture by both eminent and emerging scholars, this work is devoted to a nascent Choctaw literature, being essentially a collection of modern works (plus two from the nineteenth century).

It is likely that when readers hear the term "American Indian literature" they think of professional Native American authors who write about the Native American experience in the English language. Or they may think of trickster tales, origins myths, animal and hero stories: stories that have a tradition behind them that may be generations old. In truth, few such stories survive in Choctaw: in times past the Choctaw people tended to tell days-long epics, a style that has not continued into the present, or to sing. Indeed, much of present-day Choctaw language is retained in songs, particularly hymns: groups of Choctaws regularly get together to sing for as long as their voices will sustain them.

Here we have attempted something ambitious. Professor Haag was fascinated by Henry Willis's anecdotes about his early life, and together we hit upon the idea of collecting, not folktales, but the life stories of Choctaw people. The stories appear in both Choctaw and English; in some cases we have been privileged to find writers of both languages, and in other cases, the works have been translated. The reader who knows

Choctaw people or who lives in a Choctaw family will note immediately the perfect pitch of the authors' voices—the humor, the straightforward manner of speech, the conditions of life, particular families' ways of speaking. Just as the delightful rabbit and opossum stories were teaching tools in their day, we hope that the people who emerge from these stories will also inspire a powerful response.

Most of these selections are in fact memoirs. The contributors tell about their own lives and the lives of their relatives, both generally—describing the way they lived—and specifically, relating a memorable experience or two. All the "characters" in these stories are real Choctaw people.

It is impossible to express the gratitude we feel to our contributors for sharing precious and personal details of their lives with us, and ultimately with you.

Eveline Battiest Steele writes about country life in the mid-twentieth century, paying particular attention to her mother, Elsie Battiest, who was a monolingual Choctaw speaker and renowned basket weaver.

Jay McAlvain and his cousin Lois McAlvain Pugh share several delightful anecdotes about family members. For one, they are cousins to Neva McAlvain Bryan, who was something of a folk legend in southeastern Oklahoma, and this volume includes no fewer than three stories about her (there are many, many others!). Mrs. Pugh also tells about their grandmother Louiza McAlvain, a Cherokee woman who married into a Choctaw family and was possibly the most exciting woman in Choctaw country in the late nineteenth century.

Bill Nowlin shares the deeply moving story of his uncle Hank Brown, who was wounded grievously in World War II and successfully treated by his Choctaw grandmother.

The well-known Choctaw folklorist Tim Tingle generously allowed us access to his many stories and introductions to many Choctaw people. He also shares with us one of the "Aunt Neva" stories.

Grayson Noley, a professor of educational leadership at the University of Oklahoma and a wonderful storyteller, gives us a glimpse into Choctaw humor with his description of *ahollopi*, grave houses, and the creative uses to which they might be put.

Besides memoirs, there are three poems, some of the very few in the Choctaw language. One was written in the nineteenth century by William McKinney (kindly appearing through the courtesy of the University of Oklahoma Western History Collections). Another is by Phillip Carroll

Morgan, a known poet of Choctaw-Chickasaw heritage who is a former Choctaw language student at the University of Oklahoma and currently studying for his doctorate. Mr. Morgan learned the language as an adult and chose to express his thoughts and feelings in Choctaw; it is our hope that poetry will likewise spring up in other students as they learn the language and are moved to put their own feelings and impressions into this beautiful tongue.

We have also reproduced, transliterated, and translated a nineteenth-century pastoral letter from the Reverend Rainey (Rannie) Winthrop to Alfred (Alfol) Folsom.

Finally, there appears a second story of Lady, Henry Willis's dog, whose brave rescue of the author as a child was recounted in volume 1 of this series. This story describes the conditions of the author's young life during the Great Depression as a way of concluding the volume on the same emotional note that ended the story section in volume 1.

The Grammar

To read the stories in this volume, one must first learn the grammar. It is important to point out that this volume continues directly from volume 1, *Choctaw Language and Culture: Chahta Anumpa.* Thus, this volume includes no review of topics covered in that volume except for one short review of subject markers at the end of chapter 1. The glossaries do not repeat words found in volume 1, nor do the index and glossary of terms repeat those of volume 1.

Again, this book is intended to be used in a classroom setting with a Choctaw teacher to create other important learning experiences for the student: oral comprehension, pronunciation, speaking, and culture. The book is intended to help teachers and students understand how the language works and to give grammatically complex, high-level texts that will give real examples of the language. We understand that many students of the language will not have the privilege of working with a speaker-teacher, and we believe that the book will be of value to those who will use alternative ways of hearing the language, such as tapes and CDs.

The grammar takes on several important advanced topics and divides them into discrete and, we hope, manageable lessons. There are only twelve topics here, compared to twenty-four in volume 1, but these topics are quite abstract, and the student will want to pore over them. They include the ways that the Choctaw language is fundamentally different from English. Another important topic is that of negation, always an abstract notion but one that permeates the language at all levels—word, phrase, clause, and idiom—and is manifested in many grammatical particles. We have also selected to focus on particular kinds of usage. For example, we show how to express the notion of "never" as part of a group of related ideas. Another big topic in Choctaw is "definiteness." Again, we have tried to show how this idea conveyed is expressed in the many Choctaw definite particles.

One of the challenges that we have taken on in a serious way in this volume is explaining the many ways that a single Choctaw word can be modified to yield many subtle differences in meaning. This can be seen in the translations, where the addition of a prefix or suffix can subtly modify the meaning of the whole phrase.

Despite all the work we have poured into this volume, we remain abashed at the fact that, in truth, the work will never end. There will never be enough examples or enough explanation. But now we must turn our work into the world and allow students to profit from it as they can. The reader should know that we are fully aware of our shortcomings with respect to completeness of explanation. There are so many idioms, and so little time!

Our hope is that the student will begin to see the logic: Choctaw is fully consistent with itself. One begins to see how the words are put together and how certain particles work to produce a certain effect, even when we never say such things that way in English. Gradually, one's "Choctaw brain," as we call it, begins to take shape and develop.

Organization

This volume is organized in virtually the same way as is volume 1, with the same subsections. We begin with a selection of literature, which is then translated, loosely. We have chosen to go for artistic style rather than word-for-word glossing, which is tedious to read. Those authors who write in both languages have made translations as they deem appropriate.

A grammar section, *Anumpa vlhpesa*, follows each literature section. Next, vocabulary words, *Anumpa*, are introduced, most of them from the selected Choctaw text, along with a pronunciation guide and definition. Since there is often more than one authoritative way to spell Choctaw words, we have given alternative spellings when this makes sense. The definition is not as complete as that of a dictionary, but it is intended to give the reader the best short meaning for that word, either in the context of the text used or in general.

The word study section, *Anumpa Anukfilli*, examines specific word usage and formation more closely. It includes examination of idioms and sets of related expressions. It might be considered a secondary grammar section, one concerned with the use of words rather than the organization of clauses and phrases.

A section of exercises, *Abvchi*, gives the classroom teacher a starting point for practice. These exercises are more open-ended than those in volume 1 and require that the student be able to think about how Choctaw works rather than depending on brute-force memorization and translation. The student is often asked to rework the Choctaw selection. This is because there are so many ways the same phrase can be rendered; the student is asked to think about the Choctaw meaning and how best to express it.

Two glossaries, one Choctaw-English, the other English-Choctaw, are provided to help the student gain quick access to words that have been introduced in the text. We remind the reader that the glossaries are in no way a substitute for a good dictionary. Again, only new vocabulary words from this volume appear in the glossaries.

Orthography

There is never a completely satisfactory way to spell things. How-ever, there are several authoritative ways to spell Choctaw words and to put together compound words. With a nod toward these orthographies, we have for the most part retained the orthography introduced in volume 1. When it is possible to do so without sacrificing clarity, we have made a few changes in that orthography, hoping to simplify it and make it look more like others to which the reader will be exposed. The biggest change is that we have eliminated a number of the hyphens that connect grammatical markers with their substantive units. For example, the subject marker *vt* no longer appears connected to its noun phrase, nor does *kvt* to its clause. We believe that these markers are so familiar that readers will recognize their usage immediately. We have, however, retained the hyphens that connect person markers to their verbs, since there is far more chance for confusion with this set of forms. Some grammatical particles, such as *hosh*, have been written separately because this is customary in Choctaw writing, even though it isn't perfectly justifiable linguistically.

The predicative marker *h* is used as in volume 1: it is not written as a present tense marker except when it joins other particles or marks a dependent clause. Teachers and students from other spelling traditions may wish to use the *h* marker overtly.

As for the "aspirated *l*" (the lateral fricative), we have clung to the spelling *lh* in all instances, even though many writers use both *lh* and *hl*. The exception is in the original work of Eveline Battiest Steele, who prefers the *hl* spelling in some words; these instances have been noted for the reader. Since Choctaw has both the aspirated *l* and the consonant sequence *h-l*, in written work there is no good way to distinguish the correct sound unless the aspirated *l* is spelled the same way everywhere.

Acknowledgments

Finally, we wish to thank the many patient people who have waited a very long time for this book to be written. Our spouses, Carole Willis and Eddie Baron, must certainly be among the happiest to see this book appear. The instructional staff at the University of Oklahoma have encouraged us the whole time. The editors at the University of Oklahoma Press have been ever encouraging and enthusiastic. Special thanks to William Welge, Chester Cowen, and Terry Zinn at the Oklahoma Historical Society for helping with boxes and boxes of old manuscripts and allowing us to reproduce unique photographs. The personnel at the University of Oklahoma Western History Collections have been unfailingly helpful and speedy in helping to reproduce historical Choctaw documents.

The Choctaw community in Henning, Tennessee, merit special thanks for their contribution to vocabulary items and grammatical structure. Among them are Curtis and Lacey Bell, Verdie Mae Robinson, Eleanor Fowler, Nancy Farmer, and Wilma Lambert.

We also owe a deep debt of gratitude to our forebears, the countless people who created and nurtured the language we know today. As author Henry Willis notes, "As a young person, I was impressed by my Choctaw relatives'—aunts', cousins', uncles', as well as parents'—deep knowledge of the language. They would gently correct my speech, 'This is what he means,' they would say, so that I could overhear the right way.

"These lessons didn't impress me til much later, when I began to recall those early lessons and tried to study them. My parents never spoke English in the home. Even though I was forced to refrain from speaking Choctaw in boarding school, I was fortunate enough to return to my Choctaw-speaking family every year so that I could maintain my language."

MARCIA HAAG
Norman, Oklahoma
HENRY WILLIS
Moore, Oklahoma

Choctaw Language and Culture

CHAPTER 1

Pichukka 'Our House'

Choctaw Text and Translation: Pichukka 'Our House', by Eveline Battiest Steele

In this selection, Eveline Battiest Steele describes her early life in southeastern Oklahoma in the 1950s. Mrs. Steele is the daughter of the well-known basket maker Elsie Battiest, who spoke only Choctaw all her life. Mrs. Steele is herself a basket maker, a teacher, and a fine speaker of Choctaw.

Chukka itabana, aboha achvffa illa yo, Svshki micha Aki yvt wihvt chukkoa tok. Himmako, ahoponi aboha micha anusit aiasha aboha yo achakvli yohmi tok. Yohmi ho Pokni vt wihvt ibachukkoa tok. Aboha tuklo mvt achaka ma, chukka itabana aboha mvto Pokni imaboha toba tok. Chukka aboha tuchina asha yvmmako si-aivlhpoa tok. vlla aiushta ont ishtaiopi siah. Mak fokalih ma, svtibapishi tuchina mvto holisso apisa ont maya tok. Atoko afvmmi untuklo keyukmvt untuchina siah ma, hapichukka atokla kvt toba tok. Hapichukka asha, pimoshi, micha pikana yohmi kvt itapelvt chukka pim-ikbi tok. Chukka kanimampo keyu oka abichili keyukmvt pvla vlhtaha keyu ketok. Yohmih atoko, "chukka haiaka hikia" oklah e-hochifo tok. Himmak nittak oh mako, hopaki il-asha bieka toka, "chukka haiaka hikia" e-hochifo.

Pim oka yvt piyakni kvli hikia aminti tok. Kvli kanohmona hosh hiohmaya, mihma achvffa kano iti bvsha itabani hielichit kashoffi na oka il-ishko bieka tok. Oka ma bichelit ochi cha halvllit chukka isht ia attok.

3

Nanachefa nittak onak mano, svshki yvt ochit oka ḻawa halvllit iyasha
apittvt wahlvllichi cha toksvlit fokka achefa attok. Hokak osh nittak inlak
mano, kvli il-ia cha e-nachefa bieka tok. Itafalamoa kvt kanohmona hosh
nafohka achefa shalit atakohchi takohlichi na shila tok, anoti nittak
shohbichik ma̱, nafohka shila takohmaya ma̱ aiowa beka tok.

Osapa chito mvt illimpa moma chohmi ka̱ atahli tok. Tanchi, ahe,
tobi, hato̱fvlaha, issitushi, issito holba, shukshi, micha okchak vt osapa
aholokchi attok. Takkon ilaiyukali, takkon hochito, takkonushi, o̱kof, iti
kvfi yohmi—takkon vpi holokchi micha nukshopa itatuklo kvt osapa
apotaka afolo̱ta bieka tok. Nawaya micha takkon ḻawa kvt hvshtula vpachi̱
ho̱ olhkvchi attok. Nachampuli, walakshi, palvska micha palvska champuli yohmi kvt takkon micha takkonushi olhkvchi atoba tok.

Holisso apisa vmmona kvt chukka chaha itontalaha atukla, lukfi nuna
humma isht atoba attok. Afvmmi tuklo onah ma, holisso apisa himmona
hosh vlhtaha na e-chukkoa tok. Chukka chaha itontalaha tuklo mvt achvffa
hikivt untuchina hlopullit apisa attok. vlla holissopisa shali yvmmvt kowi
achvffa foka ho̱ chukka biḻika ant falama bieka tok. A̱ki yvt toksvlit iak mvt
holissopisa shali aiyokopa yo̱ ont-sa-kanchi cha ia tok ma̱ opiaka ma̱ akka̱ya
hosh chukka ia-lih bieka tok. Himmak kvt taha kano, satibapishi vlheha yvt
holisso apisa inla ho̱ ilhkoli attok. Satibapishi vlheha yvt holisso apisa isht
ia foka̱li mano vlla shali yvt mishema hopaki kvt kowi tuklo foka i̱shahli ho̱
yokopa bieka tok. Nahullo i̱chukka yo̱ afolota attok. Hvshtula hvshi ta̱kla
kano i̱chukka anuka binili-lachi̱ ka̱ a̱-panaklo bieka tok. Hopaki fehna kiyo
kash, nahullo ohoyo yvmma aha̱klo-li tuk.

My mother and father moved into a one-room log house. Later, another
bedroom/living room combination and kitchen were added. Then
Grandma moved in with them. After the two rooms were added, the log
room became Grandma's room. I was born in this three-room house. I
was the youngest of four children. By then, my three older brothers were
in boarding school. Then, when I was seven or eight years old, our second
home was built. Our family, uncles, and friends together helped build
our house. Neither home had running water or electricity. Therefore, we
called it our "country home." Even today, we call the old home place
"country home."

Our water came from a spring on our land. There were several
springs and one was boxed in with lumber and always kept clean for our
drinking water. The water was drawn in a bucket and carried to the house.
On wash day, many buckets of water were hauled to put in the cauldron

to boil water to wash work clothes. Other days, we went down to the spring to wash. Several trips were made to carry the washed clothes to hang on a clothesline and dry. At the end of the day, the dry clothes were collected from the clothesline.

The large garden provided most of the food. Corn, potatoes, beans, onions, squash, cucumbers, watermelons, and cantaloupes were grown in the garden. Fruit trees, both wild and domestic, lay out from the garden: large plums, apples, wild plums, persimmons, and even sassafras. Many of the vegetables and fruits were canned for eating in winter. Sweets such as dumplings, breads, and cakes were made from the canned peaches and plums.

My first school was a two-story red brick building. Two years later, the new school building was completed and we moved into it. The two-story building housed grades one through eight. The school bus came to about a mile from my home. My Dad dropped me off at the bus stop on his way to work, but in the evening I walked home. By this time, my brothers were at another boarding school. When my brothers started school, the school bus stopped even farther out—about two miles. The turnaround was at the home of a white family. During the winter months, they invited me into their home. I heard from that white lady not long ago.

Eveline Battiest Steele

Note: Mrs. Steele uses some common spelling variations that differ in small ways from those that appear elsewhere in this book. These are noted for the reader's convenience: untuklo (ontuklo), untuchina (ontuchina), pim oka (pimoka), wahlᵥllichi (walhᵥllichi), hlopullit (lhipullit). The -t form of verbs ending in -a is -ᵥt instead of -at, as in wihᵥt, itapelᵥt, and apittᵥt.

Anumpa ᵥlhpesa (Grammar): Indicating *Self* and *Each Other*

Choctaw, like many American Indian languages, forms verbs made of several particles (or markers), each of which carries information. Choctaw verbs are thus not put together in the way English verbs are. The student is probably already familiar with many of these particles: the tense markers, such as *-h*, *tuk*, and *-achi*; the mood markers, such as *-ahe*, *ahinla*, and *ahekeyu*; and the person markers. There are many more of these particles that add other important meanings to Choctaw verbs. In this chapter we will introduce particles that give the sense of the English *oneself, each other, together,* and *with* (in the sense of accompaniment).

The Reflexive Markers *ile* and *ila*

Reflexive person markers, which in English are pronouns such as *myself, yourselves, himself, itself,* and so forth, are used to show that the subject of a verb performs some action upon itself. Another way to state this is to say that the subject and object are the same person. In the following set of English examples, notice that the reflexive pronoun matches the subject and tells us that the subject is performing the action of the verb upon itself.

John hurt himself.
I see myself in the mirror.
You probably can't hear yourselves in this din.

In Choctaw, the reflexive marker that corresponds to these English forms is *ile*: unlike the English forms, it does not change each time we name a different person. We know who the person is by the form of the subject person marker. Like most other Choctaw person markers, the reflexive *ile* is bound to the verb, meaning it does not appear apart from the verb. Most spelling traditions attach *ile* directly to the left side of the verb stem, after the subject marker. When *ile* appears before a verb that begins with a short vowel, one of the vowels is deleted, sometimes the *-e-* and other times the following vowel, in the same fashion as we have seen with other markers.

a. Ish-ilehaksichih-o̱?
   Are you deceiving yourself?
b. Meli-ʋt ilachefa.
   Mary is washing herself. (The *e* from *ile* is deleted.)
c. Oklah ilachefa.
   They are washing themselves.
d. Hattak ilbʋsha mʋt ilebi tuk.
   That poor man killed himself. (The *ʋ* from *ʋbi* is deleted.)

Reflexives That Mark the Recipient Person or Other Objects

Besides marking the person who is directly affected by the action of a verb, a reflexive can also mark the *recipient*, what in English is usually the indirect object, of a verb, as well as other roles such as the person who benefits from an action (benefactive) and the source of something. Notice in the following English examples that the reflexive pronoun tells us that the subject and the recipient are the same. In English, these are often marked with the prepositions *to, of, from,* and *about.* If you find it hard to tell if something is directly affected by the verb, or is a recipient, try using one of these prepositions to make the distinction.

> Hedy bought herself a new hat. (Hedy bought a new hat **for herself.**)
> I was forced to laugh **at myself.**
> We paid ourselves fifty dollars each. (We paid fifty dollars each **to ourselves.**)

In Choctaw, of course, the recipient object is always distinguished by a separate form. The reflexive marker that corresponds to the recipient is *ila* and its variant form *ilai,* used when the next sound, on the verb, is *y.* When the verb begins with a vowel, the speaker may delete the *-a-* (forming *il-*). Again, *ila* is not marked to distinguish different persons; we know who the recipient is because it is the same as the subject. *Ila-,* and its variants *il-* and *ilai-,* are attached directly to the verb stem, after the person markers.

> a. Ilhpak moma ka ilaieshi tuk.
>   He took all the food to himself. (*ilai + ishi* 'get')
> b. Iti lumbo ya hash-ilahallvlli.
>   You are pulling the log to yourselves.

An important idiom using *ila* is the one corresponding to the English *buy for oneself.* Here, we use the *-t* form of *chompa* (see chapter 11 in *Choctaw Language and Culture*) plus *ilahabinlachi* 'give to oneself' — or literally 'buy and give to oneself'.

> Sholush himona chompat ilahabinlachi-li tuk.
> I bought myself new shoes. (I bought new shoes for myself.)

Isht ile, Isht ila

We sometimes need to express other kinds of objects besides the ones expressed with *ile* and *ila. Isht ile* and *isht ila* are used when an instrument is mentioned or implied. It is also the idiom for the English 'talk about oneself'.

   a. Isht ilechạli-tuk.
      He cut himself (with an axe). (Literally, "He chopped himself.")
   b. Chani-ѵt isht ilanumpuli.
      Johnny is talking about himself.

The Reciprocal Markers *iti*, *itim*, and *ita*

The set of *reciprocal* person markers gives us the sense of the English phrase *each other*. *Iti-* is attached to the left side of the verb stem, after the person markers, if any. It always refers to plural persons, of course.

   a. Hattak micha ohoyo-ѵt itipisa tuk.
      The man and woman looked at each other.
   b. Alikchi-ѵt itiapelah beka.
      Doctors always help each other.
   c. Hash-itihạkloh-ọ?
      Do you hear each other?
   d. Pi-ѵllah mah, il-itilhioli kѵt pim-achukma tok.
      When we were children, we liked to chase each other.

The student will notice that *iti*, like *ile*, marks objects that are directly affected by the verb.

Reciprocal Objects That Are Also Recipients

In English, we can use the expressions *to each other* and *for each other*, along with other expressions such as *about each other*, *from each other*, and the like. In Choctaw we mark this usage with the reciprocal form *itim*, which will be pronounced and spelled *itị* when it appears before consonants, something that should be very familiar to the student by now. Again, since these objects are not easily distinguished in English, students should try using an appropriate preposition (*to, about, for*) if they are not clear whether the reciprocal is affected or recipient. Examine these English examples first:

We were speaking to each other.
We gave each other nice gifts. (We gave nice gifts **to each other**.)
They told each other a lot of lies. (They told a lot of lies **to each other**.)

In Choctaw, *itim* or its variant *iti̲* appears directly before the verb stem.

a. Pilashash a̲kana micha vno yvt il-itimanumpuli tuk.
   Yesterday my friends and I were talking to each other.
b. Pi̲kana yvt iti̲nukoa.
   Our friends are angry with each other.
c. Ohoyo sipokni vlheha mvt nananoa itimanolih bieka.
   Those old women are always telling each other stories.
d. Hattak moma yvmmvt itimi̲kana.
   All those men are friends with each other.
e. A̲kanomi vt itimanumpuli kvt im-achukma.
   My relatives like to talk to each other.

One idiom, *ilitimanumpuli*, 'talking to oneself', puts together *ila* plus *itim*, literally meaning 'talking together to oneself':

vllanakni ossi mvt ilitimanumpulit binili.
That little boy is sitting talking to himself.

Ita 'Together'

A commonly used Choctaw particle that is included in the set with *iti* and *itim* is *ita*, which is not strictly a reciprocal but does give the meaning of the English 'together'. *Ita* always makes a verb plural or is used with plural forms. For many speakers, *ita* may not be used to indicate dual number (exactly two persons). We have already seen this marker used in many words, such as *itanowa* 'walk together'. Again, *ita* appears before the verb stem after the person markers.

a. vllanakni ushta mvt chukka palhki hosh itanowa.
   Those four boys are walking quickly together to the house.
b. Peni il-itatakchichi.
   We tied the boats together.
c. "Hapi̲chukka asha, pimoshi, micha pi̲kana yohmi kvt itapelat chukka pim-ikbi tok."
   Our family, uncles, friends and such together helped to build our house. (Readers may notice that this translation is not exactly the same as that found in the Choctaw text at the beginning of this

chapter. These differences, and others throughout the text, illustrate the many possible ways of translating a given sentence.)

The Accompaniment Marker *iba*

We have already learned how to the use instrumental *isht*, which corresponds to the English *with*. Another kind of *with* is that which signifies accompaniment. Accompaniment is marked with *iba* and its variant *ibai*, which is used before vowels. The second syllable, *-a-*, is always long in this marker. *Iba* very often appears with *ita* to form *itiba* 'together with'. Again, *iba* appears after the person markers before the verb stem.

   a. "Yohmi họ Pokni ʋt wihat ibachukkoa tok."
      And so, Grandma moved in with them.
   b. Chi'baiʋla ka̱ pịsa-li tuk.
      I saw that he arrived with you.
   c. Sa'baimpah chi-bʋnnah-ọ?
      Do you want to dine with me?
   d. Hattak ʋt itibatanohọwa tuk.
      The men were walking together in a group.

ANUMPA (Vocabulary)

Vocabulary words are listed alphabetically by part of speech. A pronunciation guide follows each new word. An accented syllable means that that syllable is to receive stress. Words without accents receive even stress.

Nouns

ʋlla holissopisa shali	[ʋl-lʋ ho-lis-so-pi-sʋ shá-li]	school bus
afolota	[a-fo-ló-tʋ]	turnaround
aholisso apisa	[a-ho-lis-so a-pí-sʋ]	school building
aiithana ʋlhi	[ai-i-ta-nʋ ʋ-lhi]	memoir
apisa	[a-pí-sʋ]	lesson; grade in school
atakohchi	[a-ta-kóh-chi]	clothesline
chukka asha	[chuk-ká-shʋ]	family
chukka itabana	[chuk-kʋ i-tʋ-bá-nʋ]	log house

ishtochi	[isht-ó-chi]	bucket
issito holba	[is-si-to-hól-bv]	cucumber
issitushi	[is-si-tú-shi]	squash
iti kvfi	[i-ti k'v́-fi]	sassafras tree
iti lumbo	[i-ti ló-bu]	log
itontalaha	[i-to-tv-lá-ha]	story; floor (of building)
iyasha	[i-yá-shv]	iron cauldron
kvli	[kv-li]	spring (of water); well
kowi	[kó-wi]	mile
lukfi nuna	[luk-fi nú-nv]	brick
nanalhto	[na-nálh-tu]	container; bucket
ochak	[ó-chvk]	cantaloupe
oka abicheli	[o-kv a-bi-ché-li]	running water
okof	[ó-kuf]	persimmon
opiaka	[o-pí-yv-ka]	evening
pvla vlhtaha	[pv-lv vlh-tá-ha]	electric lights
shukshi	[shúk-shi]	watermelon
takohmaya	[ta-koh-má-yv]	clothesline
walakshi	[wv-lák-shi]	Choctaw dumplings

Verbs

Verbs marked "Gp. 2" (Group 2) have affected subjects; verbs marked "Gp. 3" (Group 3) have recipient subjects. Unmarked verbs are "Gp. 1" (Group 1) and have agent subjects. See the final section of this chapter, *Ish-ikhaiyanah momah-o?*, for a review of person markers.

achaka	[a-cha-kv]	be added to; united (Gp. 2)
achakvli	[a-cha-kv-li]	add to; unite
aivlhpa	[ai-vlh-pv]	be born somewhere (Gp. 2)
akkaya	[ak-ka-yv]	go on foot
apitta	[a-pit-tv]	put plural things into something
bicheli	[bi-che-li]	draw liquid from a container
itabvni	[i-ta-bv-ni]	put together by fitting pieces
itabana	[i-ta-ba-nv]	be fit into each other (a log house)
nachefa	[na-che-fv]	do the wash; launder

ochi	[o-chi]	draw water with a bucket from well
takohlichi	[ta-koh-li-chi]	hang up plural things
walhvllichi	[wa-lhvl-li-chi]	cause to boil

Adjectives

vmmona	[v́m-mo-nv]	first
imoma	[i-mo-mv]	natural
ishtaiopi	[isht-ái-yo-pi]	last
kanomona, kanohmona	[ka-no-mó-nv]	several; many
olhkvchi, ulhkvchi	[ulh-kv-chi]	canned; soaked; steeped

Adverbs

mishema	[mi-she-mv]	farther; farther off
takla	[tak-lv]	during; while
yohmi	[yoh-mi]	be so; and such

Idioms

achvffa hikiat untuchina lhipullit apisa	grades one through eight
chukka chaha itontalaha tuklo	two-story building
chukka haiaka hikia	country home
holissopisa shali aiyokopa	school bus stop
kowi tuklo foka ishahli ho	about two miles more
ont-sa-kanchi	leave me off

Anumpa Anukfilli (Word Study): Words Containing Reflexive and Reciprocal Markers

There are a number of vocabulary words that are made with the markers introduced in this lesson. Look at the following list of words and note, when you can, how the meanings can be related to the meanings of the parts. Sometimes, as in all languages, the final meaning of the word has become somewhat different than the original meanings of the parts.

| itichukka | spouse |
| itipesa | interview |

itaisso	clash
ilahnichi	self-esteem
ilaiyukpa	enjoy
ilefehnachi	boast
ilitahina	chums
itilaui	equal
itishi	wrestle
itahoba	congregate
ilaiyuka	diverse
ibaiyukpa	rejoice with
ileyimmi	self-confidence

Abnchi (Exercises)

Chi-anukfokah-o? (Do You Understand?)

Choose one of the paragraphs in Mrs. Steele's Choctaw memoir and translate it again, using your own words. Notice how many different ways we can say the same thing. Are there parts of your translation that you like better?

Anumpa vlhpesa (Grammar)

A. Translate each sentence to Choctaw, using reflexive markers. Pay attention to the role of the objects: are they directly affected by the action of the verb, or are they recipients?

1. He hit himself.
2. We helped ourselves.
3. I cut myself (with a knife).
4. You got it for yourself.
5. They bought it for themselves.
6. She is talking to herself.

B. Translate the following to Choctaw, using the reciprocal markers. Again, pay attention to the type of object each sentence uses.

1. We helped each other.
2. They looked at each other.
3. You spoke to each other.

4. We looked for each other.
5. They laughed at each other.
6. You hugged each other.
7. They brought it to each other.

C. Translate to Choctaw using *ita-*, *iba-* or *itiba-* in the verb.

1. We went to town together.
2. They ate with us.
3. We danced together.
4. Did you leave together?
5. They watched television with you.

D. What do these sentences mean?

1. Chukka asha yvt kulli imoma itanowat ilhkoli tuk.
2. Shukshi moma ka ilaieshi-lachi.
3. Svshki micha A̲ki vt iti̲hullo.

Holissochi (Writing)

Write a short story on a topic of your choice. Among your verbs, include at least one reflexive form, one reciprocal form, and one form with *ita-*, *iba-*, or *itiba-*.

Ish-ikhaiyanah momah-o̲? 'Do You Remember?'

Group 1, Group 2, and Group 3 verbs

One of the first questions a student of Choctaw must ask when learning a new verb is "What kind of subject marker does it take?" All Choctaw verbs belong to one of three groups, each of which takes a different kind of subject: *agent* subjects (Group 1), *affected* subjects (Group 2), and *recipient* subjects (Group 3). Of course, this is only important when we need to use person markers (the particles that correspond to pronouns in English). Most verbs take agent subjects: the subject of the verb is doing something. Another large group of verbs, and all adjective predicates, have affected subjects: the subject of the verb or predicate is in some state or condition. A few verbs have recipient subjects: these subjects are generally the experiencer of some sensation or psychological condition.

Table 1 is a chart of some common verbs and their subject markers.

TABLE 1
Common Verbs and their Subject Markers

Subject Agreement for Group 1 Verbs (Agent)	Subject Agreement for Group 2 Verbs (Affected)	Subject Agreement for Group 3 Verbs (Recipient)
balili-li 'I run'	sa-bʋnna 'I want'	am-anukfila 'I think'
ish-balili 'you run'	chi-bʋnna 'you want'	chim-anukfila 'you think'
balili 'he, she, they run'	bʋnna 'he, she, they want'	im-anukfila 'he, she, they think'
e-balili 'we run'	pi-bʋnna 'we want'	pim-anukfila 'we think'
eho-balili 'we all run'	hapi-bʋnna 'we all want'	hapim-anukfila 'we all think'
hash-balili 'you (pl.) run'	hachi-bʋnna 'you (pl.) want'	hachim-anukfila 'you (pl.) think'
akostinichi-li 'I recollect'	si-anukfohka 'I understand'	a̱-hiki̱a 'I have (something large)'
ish-akostinichi 'you recollect'	chi-anukfohka 'you understand'	chi̱-hiki̱a 'you have'
akostinichi 'he,she, they recollect'	anukfohka 'he, she, they understand'	i̱-hiki̱a 'he, she, they have'
il-akostinichi 'we recollect'	pi-anukfohka 'we understand'	pi̱-hiki̱a 'we have'
iloh-akostinichi 'we all recollect'	hapi-anukfohka 'we all understand'	hapi-hiki̱a 'we all have'
hash-akostinichi 'you (pl.) recollect	hachi-anukfohka 'you pl. understand'	hachi̱-hiki̱a 'you pl. have'

CHAPTER 2

Hopakih Chash Yakohmih Beka Tok
'How They Did It in the Old Days'

Choctaw Text and Translation: *Hopakih Chash Yakohmih Beka Tok*
'How They Did It in the Old Days', by Eveline Battiest Steele

Eveline Battiest Steele continues with her recollections of her early life in southeastern Oklahoma. Here she talks about basket weaving and old-fashioned Choctaw hospitality.

Pokni yvt afvmmi pokoli tuklo mvt tapushik tvnna ipunna tok, miya. Yohmi kia, si-vllah moma kvt, Pokni ihohchifo alhi yvt Fannie ya ak-ikhano bieka tok. Pokni oshitek tuklo micha oshitek ippochihoyo ma tapushik ikbi im-abahanchi tok. Oshitek ittatuklo kvt tapushik ikbi ipunnvt taha tok. Pokni yvt afvmmih tahlepa sipokni vbih chakkali cha pokoli hvnnali akucha chakkali (1969) yvmma illi tok; akinli kia afvmmih tahlepa sipokni pokoli ushta takla ma ik-peso toba cha tapushik ikbit issa tok. Afvmmi tahlepa sipokni pokoli untuchina micha pokoli chakkali takla ka Oklahoma Chahta ohoyo tuchina ilvppak illa hosh tapushik ikbi ipunna yosh Oklahoma Chahta anoa tok. Afvmmi pokoli chakkali chukovt isht ia ma, vno (Pokni ippok vllatek) akosh svshki tapushik ikbi im-aiikhanvt isht ia-li tok. Atokkosh, afvmmi kanohmona, anoti svshki yvt illih ma, sioshi Corey (Pokni ippok nakni chito) akosh Chahta itapushik nanaivlhto yo ikbit tok. Himak nittak a, ohoyo tuchina mvt tapushik ikbit toka, Nasipokni Aiasha ilaiyukvt hiohmayvt yakni hlopulli ka, asha na ish-ahochahinla.

Sa-hofantit vtta-lih ma, Chahta Anumpa mak illa ho chukka asha yvt okla itimanumpuli bieka tok. Hapikana keyukmvt chukkapanta asha

Elsie Battiest teaches her daughter Eveline Steele to weave traditional Choctaw baskets in her home in Broken Bow, Oklahoma, in 1989. The bottom of the basket is square or rectangular, but the sides will be raised to become round or oblong. Traditionally, dyes were made from berries, roots, and minerals, but today analine dyes are used. Note Mrs. Battiest's dress and apron, and her manner of arranging her hair. This style of dress is seldom seen today. *Courtesy of the Oklahoma Historical Society.*

kanimampo kvt nowat ayvt pichukka vlak mvt Chahta Anumpa illa anumpulih bieka tok. Svshki micha itek vt tapushik itibatvnna keyukmvt nittak hullo itibahoponih aiyukalik mvt Chahta bieka ho itimanumpuli attok. Chahta Babil hochefo micha Chahta Vba Isht Talowa svshki yvt chitoli hosh talohowat binilit foha bieka tok. Chahta talowa talohowat im atoksvli isht ahanta tok. Svppokni ato talovt anta ka ak-haklo ket tok, amba svshki ato talohowa billia attok. Svshki haklot sv-hofanti kakosh vba isht talowa anumpa lawa ka ikhvna-li tuk. Talohowvt nittak ont ai isht im-aiyopit illi tok. Hvklo-li hokakosh, ak-ibatalowo ket tok. Himmak ako, ibatalowa-li tok mato ahni-li.

  Hopak kash o nowvt ayvt chukka ant chukkovt binili makinli ho, nanishko keyukmvt nana kia ipeta beka tok. Himak ano, kana ikana chiyyohmit nan imatahli yohmi ka e-pisah fehna keyu. Ninak lawa ho svshki vt ninak iklvnna keyukmvt hvshi kanvlli tuklo keyukmvt tuchina tani cha nahinli impa palvska keyukmvt palvska alwvsha, akakushi lobochi micha bota bila isht ashela hoponi ka pisa-li beka tok. Ahoponi vt libesha taklah ma palvska himo ikbih beka tok. Kafi himo ikbi tok. Kanihmik ma falamvt ik-nuso ket tok. Nowvt ayah mvt pikanomi keyukmvt hapimoshi yosh pashpoa toba keyukmvt ponola osapa atoksvlit vtta tok osh ichukka ia hosh aya bieka tok. Hvshi kanvlli kanihmi kia ant pinowvt ayah bekak mvt, impa hinla kvt ikhana tok.

Grandma was a master basket weaver at the age of twenty. Grandma's name was Fannie, although I didn't know that when I was young. Grandma taught her two daughters and one of her daughter's sisters-in-law basketry. The daughters became master artists in basketry. Grandma died in 1969 but had gone blind during the 1940s and had to give up basketry. In the eighties and nineties, these three women were known as the only master artists among the Oklahoma Choctaws. Then in the early nineties, I (Fannie's granddaughter) started learning the art from my mother. A few years later, when Mother died, my son Corey (Fannie's great-grandson) made a Choctaw storage basket. Today, baskets made by the three women may be found across the country in various museums.

The household spoke only the Choctaw language when I was growing up. Our visiting friends or neighbors who came to our home spoke only Choctaw. Every time Mom and her sister got together to weave baskets or bake for holidays, they spoke the language. The Choctaw Bible was read and the Choctaw hymns sung aloud as my mother sat down to rest. She often sang Choctaw hymns as she went about doing her household chores. I didn't hear Grandma singing, but my mother sang often. I learned the words to many of the hymns by listening to Mother. She sang until the day she died. I listened, but I didn't sing along. Now I wish that I had sung with her.

A long time ago, as soon as a visitor sat down, they were brought something to drink or eat. We don't often see that kind of hospitality today. Many nights, I have seen my mother get up in the middle of the night or at two or three o'clock in the morning to cook an early breakfast of biscuits or fried bread, eggs, and gravy. Biscuits were made from scratch while the wood cookstove was heating up the oven. Fresh coffee was made. Sometimes she did not go back to sleep. The visitors were often cousins and uncles going home from working out in the broom corn or cotton fields. They would stop off at our home because they knew they could get a meal at any hour.

Eveline Battiest Steele

Note: Mrs. Steele uses some common spelling variations of words that appear a bit differently elsewhere in this book: tahlepa (talhepa), ittatuklo (itatuklo), atokkosh (atokosh), talowa (taloa), im atoksvli (imatoksali), ket tok (ketok), nan imatahli (nanimatahli), impa hinla (impahinla). -t forms of verbs ending in -a are spelled -vt (ipunnvt, chukovt, and so forth).)

ANUMPA VLHPESA: *Yohmi*—Its Idioms and Its Compounds

A word we encounter over and over in Choctaw is *yohmi* 'to be so'. This word, a predicate, serves an important purpose in the language: it allows us to refer to something that has already been said. *Yohmi* has many compounds in Choctaw and is translated many ways into English.

Look at the uses and translations of *yohmi* in the following sentences and notice the sense of the English 'be so' in each of them.

a. "Hapichukka asha, pimoshi, micha pikana **yohmi** kvt itapelat chukka pim-ikbi tok" (from chapter 1).
All our neighbors, uncles, friends **and so forth** helped together to build our house.

b. "**Yohmi atoko**, 'chukka haiaka hikia' oklah e-hochifo tok" (from chapter 1).
Therefore, we called it our "country home."

c. "Takkon ilaiyukali, takkon hochito, takkonushi, okof, iti kvfi **yohmi**— takkon vpi holokchi micha nukshopa itatuklo kvt osapa apotaka afolota bieka tok" (from chapter 1).
Large plums, apples, wild plums, persimmon and **even** sassafras— fruit trees both wild and domestic lay out from the garden.

d. "**Yohmi kia** si-vllah moma kvt, Pokni ihohchifo alhi yvt Fannie ya ak-ikhano bieka tok."
Grandma's name was Fannie, **although** I didn't know that when I was young.

e. "**Yohmi tokvt** takali-li tuk" (from chapter 3).
Well, I got stuck.

f. "**Yohmi mvlhi hoka**, is-sam-issa ok na ak-chi-kuchi-lahinla," im-achi tok" (from chapter 3).
"**Well indeed**, if you bid me, let me get you out," he said to her.

g. "**Yohmih ma** shukvta yvt nanikayo hosh binnili nahah ma . . ." (from chapter 22, *Choctaw Language and Culture*).
So then the opossum sat there taking his time . . .

Reference to Something Already Stated

Many times in conversation we wish to connect a new statement with something we have already said. In English, we have many adverbs and conjunctions that do this work: another way we do this is with *well*, which indicates to the listener that the speaker wants to connect what he is about to say with what has already been said. In Choctaw, instead of many different expressions, we very often use *yohmi* with one of the conjunctions or subordinators, or with an adverb, to give many different nuances.

Idioms made with *yohmi*
Here is a list of some of the common and useful expressions you will find made with *yohmi*.

yohmikash	it so happened
yohmi chash	when it happened
yohmi ash	habitually did something
yohmi hosh	being so; in so doing (same subject)
yohmi ho	so it was; since
yohmi ka	as it is; therefore
yohmi cha	do it and; after doing it (same subject)
yohmi kʋt	doing it; doing so (same subject)
yohmi ato; kato	the one that did (contrastive)
yohmi hikat	if one were to
yohmih ma	when it happened

Here is a list of sentences that use idiomatic expressions with *yohmi*:

a. Pilashash yohmikash ish-ikhanah momah-o?
   Do you remember what happened yesterday?
b. Yohmi chash ish-ikhanah momah-o?
   Do you remember when it happened?
c. Hattak shali apoksia yohmi ash falamat ont ki-pisa.
   Let's go back and see the one who used to fix cars.
d. Yohmi hosh Akinsa ittiachi tok.
   And in doing so, the two went to Arkansas.
e. Yohmi ho Akinsa ittiachi tok.
   And so it was that the two went to Arkansas.
f. Ombah yohmi ho ak'lo tuk.
   Since it was raining I didn't get here.

g. Yohmi ka̲ akka itanowa hosh ilhkoli tuk.
    Therefore they went walking on foot.
h. Yohmi cha Bilhihim ayonah ma̲ afoha hoyo tok.
    They did this and they arrived in Bethlehem and looked for shelter.
i. Yohmi kʋt issahekeyu.
    He can't stop doing it.
j. Chukka kashoffi yohmi ato, i̲punnahoke.
    Whoever does the cleaning is excellent indeed.
k. Yohmi kato ilbʋsha a̲lhi.
    But the one who did is truly suffering.
l. Nana inla yohmi hikat, achukmah kiyo.
    If one should do something else, it's not good.
m. Yohmi ma̲, pi̲chukka il-ilhkoli tuk.
    When it happened, we went home.

Compounds with the *ohmi* Root

There are many words, including *yohmi*, that are made with the root *ohmi*, which means 'like'. Among them are:

ohmi	like; image
yamohmi	do like
chohmi	similar
makohmi	like that; image of
choyohmichi	do like; make like
ile-chohmichi	make oneself like
ile-choyohmichi	make oneself out as

Here is a list of sentences that contain words with the *ohmi* root:

a. ʋlla yʋt i̲ki pisah ohmi.
    The child looks like his father.
b. Hattak mʋt hattak inla yamohmi ka̲ mihchi.
    That man is doing it like the other man.
c. Hattak mʋt pisa ka̲ mak holba chohmi.
    That man looks sort of like that other man.
d. Ofi kania yʋt pisa ka̲ makohmi.
    The lost dog looks like that.

e. Hattak inla choyohmichi hosh aiasha tok.
They were doing as other people were.

f. Hattak ᴠt imanukfila iksho ile-chohmichi hosh, ia tuk.
The man, making a fool of himself, left.

g. Balili ipunna ile-choyohmichi hosh ᴠla tuk.
He came making himself out to be an expert runner.

ANUMPA

Nouns

hᴠshi kanᴠlli	[hᴠ-shi kᴠ-n'ᴠ́l-li]	hour
ippochihoyo	[ip-po-chi-hó-yu]	sister-in-law
nanimatahli	[na-ni-ma-táh-li]	hospitality; service
pashpoa	[pásh-pu-ᴠ]	broomcorn
tikba	[tík-bᴠ]	ancestors

Verbs

hofanti	[ho-fa-ti]	grow up (Gp. 2)
ibataklat aya	[i-ba-tak-lᴠt a-yᴠ]	hang around with someone
lobolichi	[lu-bo-li-chi]	boil something
yakohmi	[ya-koh-mi]	do in some fashion

Adjectives

lobochi	[lo-bo-chi]	boiled
nahinli	[na-hi-li]	early (shortening of onnahinli)

Adverbs

akkia	[ák-ki-yᴠ]	along with; also; too
illa; mak illa	[il-lᴠ]	only; alone
tikba	[tik-bᴠ]	in the beginning

Idioms

hᴠshi kanᴠlli tuklo	two o'clock
im-abahanchi	give instruction to someone
im-aiopi illa	last day; dying day

| imanukfila iksho | fool; brainless person |
| miya, miha | they say (used in stories) |

ANUMPA ANUKFILLI: First and Last—*Tikba* and *Ishtaiopi*

There are a number of Choctaw expressions, several of them related, that are used to express the notions of *first, before, last, the beginning,* and so forth.

Tikba, Tikba, Tikbali, Tikbali

The usual word for 'first' is *tikba* and its related forms. This is the adverbial meaning of *first*: beforehand in space and time. The difference between *tikba* and *tikbali* is subtle: generally, *tikbali* is used when the meaning is 'by going first'.

a. Tikbalih vla-li tuk.
   I arrived first.
b. Ish-tikbalih-o?
   Were you first?
c. vlat ish-tikbalih-o?
   Were you first to arrive?
d. Tikba pisa-li.
   I saw him before/first.
e. Pilashash tikbali pisa li tuk.
   I saw him beforehand, yesterday.
f. Aiitatoba tikba ia-li tuk.
   I went to the store first.
g. Tikbalih maka-li tuk.
   I said it in the beginning; I said it first.
h. Yvmmakosh tikba atok.
   That guy was first.

vmmona

Choctaw uses a special word to mean *the first one* or *the first time*:

a. Holisso vmmona ya e-chompa.
   We bought the first book.

Eveline Battiest Steele and a collection of Choctaw baskets that she and her mother, Elsie Battiest, wove. The patterns on the sides are typical of the southeastern area. Baskets on the table show various stages of production. Those on the wall are sifters and winnowers, important baskets for daily use. *Courtesy of the Oklahoma Historical Society.*

    b. Yvmmakosh vmmona atok.
       That guy was the first one.

Notice that in English there is very little difference in meaning between this last example and example h. above.

Ishtaiopi

    The expression for 'last' in Choctaw is the rather idiomatic verb *isht-aiopi*, also written as *isht ayopi* and *isht aiiopi*:

    a. Ishtaiopi vla-li.
       I arrived last.
    b. vllanakni ilvppakosh ishtaiopi.
       This boy is the last one.

c. ʋlla ishtaiopi ilʋppakosh salahat ʋla tuk.
This last child got here slowly.

d. Anumpa makosh im-ishtaiopi.
Those words were his last.

e. Nittak ilʋppa makosh am-ishtaiopi.
This is my last day.

f. "Talohọwat nittak ont aiisht im-aiopit illi tok."
She went on singing until the day she died (her last day).

Note in examples d., e., and f. that the recipient marker is attached to *ishtaiopi* to give the sense of *the last for someone.*

a. ʋno akosh ishtaiopi.
I am the last.

b. "ʋlla aiushta ont ishtaiopi siah" (from chapter 1).
I am the last child of four. (Literally, "I am the fourth child and the last.")

Abʋchi

Chi-anukfọkah-ọ?

Return to the first two stories in this volume and note the number of times *yohmi* appears. Show how it works in each case.

Anumpa ʋlhpesa

A. Select any five of the *yohmi* idioms and use them in sentences. Pay attention to how you translate the idioms.

B. Select any five of the *ohmi* compounds and use them in sentences. Note how the root adds to the meaning of the word.

C. What do these sentences mean?

1. Sanakfish ʋt issito holba moma ka̱ ʋpa tuk. Yohmi kʋt yʋmmʋt abekat toba tuk.

2. Tikba, pashpoa aiowa-lachi, yohmi cha lobolichi-lachi.
3. Chippochihoyo akosh ishtaiopi ona tuk.

Holissochi

Write a short memoir about some experience in your own life. Translate it to English.

CHAPTER 3

Hokni Nefa 'Aunt Neva'

Choctaw Text and Translation: *Hokni Nefa* 'Aunt Neva', by
Jay McAlvain

*There are many anecdotes and stories about the real-life resident of
LeFlore County, Oklahoma, Neva Leon McAlvain Bryan. She was born in
Wister, Indian Territory, and became affectionately known to Choctaws in
southeastern Oklahoma as "Aunt Neva," a symbol of the "country Indian":
the one who is resourceful, hard-working, and good-hearted and remains
unruffled by modern times and contraptions. Aunt Neva was famous for her
problematic relationships with automobiles, as her cousin Jay McAlvain
relates here, rendered into Choctaw by Henry Willis.*

Nefa yʋt nana inla alhi tok. Nitak achʋffa mạ, chuka chʋffa moma
kʋt oklah pisat ilhkoli tok mihma ịhattakshali ʋt peh kucha hikia tok
micha lukfi isht akmo kaniak atok. Aialhi kạ, momah lukfi isht ompoholmo kania kʋto. Tombi pisa nana akohmi kạ ish-pisa fehna hekeyu tok.
Okla aboha ont chukowat "Omikato, Nefa, nạta hosh yakni paknaka talaia
kạ chịnashali ʋt akaniohmi tok?"

"Nitak achʋffakash, ulbal abohli pila imma yʋmmakọ aiʋtta tok
yʋmma kana't mạya moma kạ ahnit pisat ia-lachị kʋt am-anukfila tok.
Peh kana kia ulbal mah mạya moma kah ahnit anukfilli-li tok. Atokọ
yʋmmimma lhipullit ạya-li tok."

Tikba nitak achʋffa keyukmʋt tuklo mah, nana kạ, omba tok atokọ
lukfi hina sipokni akkoat ʋttat nowat ạya tok. Hattakshali yạ isht ạyat pit

27

chukoa cha lukchuk chito okakⱴniat lukchuk isht ompoholmot tahli tok. Isht chanaha chanⱴlichit chanⱴlichit nana ho̲ kaniohmi kia kucha hekeyu taha tuk. Yohmi kia yⱴmmⱴt ataklama keyu tok, peh kuchat iti nutakchit ont binili cha makinli ho̲ binili na shohbi tok. Peh kucha iti nuta yⱴmma binili tok. Yohmi atukkia, opia a̲lhi tahah ma̲ hattak kan-imma kⱴt tamaha to̲ksalit ⱴtta tukosh fohah mⱴt hina inla apatat a̲ya yo̲ nachⱴfichi'sh a̲ya tok. Ma̲ yohmi kⱴt peh yohmi kⱴt filemat yⱴmma pit pisah mⱴt nana hokano pisa tok. Micha, "Yⱴmmⱴt hattakshali yosh hikia ahoba," ahnit anukfilli tok.

Yⱴmmaki̲ folotat micha ulbal ont afolota cha a̲shaka amitit ona tok. Aia̲lhi ka̲, iti nuta yⱴmmⱴt yⱴmma binili tok. Mihma, "Yakni ilⱴppa̲ katiohmi ho̲ ilⱴppa̲ ish-binili?" im-achi tok. "Yohmi tokⱴt takali-li tuk. Ilⱴppa̲ binili shoyohbih."

"Yohmi mⱴlhi hoka̲, is-sam-issa okma ak-chi-kuchi-lahinla," im-achi tok. Mihmⱴt iat osapa nanishthalⱴlli ont ishtⱴla cha atakalichit halⱴllit isht kohchi tok. Nefa yⱴt nanisht ahni keyu tok. Peh iti nuta yⱴmma binili na nitak alhipulli tok. Yohmi mⱴlhi kiyo kia, hattakshali ya̲ ik-kashoffo kesha tok. Kucha ma̲ hikia kⱴt lukfi kⱴllo isht ompoholmo moma tok.

Neva was something else. One day the whole family went to see her and her car was sitting out there and it was just caked with mud. I mean, it had mud all over it. You could hardly see what color it was. And they went in and said, "Well, Neva, what in the world has happened to your car?"

Neva said, "Oh, the other day I decided I'd go down and see if any-one still lived back in there where I used to live. . . . I grew up back there in the woods. I just wondered if anybody still lived back there. So I went down through there."

It had rained a day or two before and she got off on this old dirt road. She pulled off down in there and just buried her car. She just sat there and spun and spun, couldn't get out. But it didn't bother Neva. She just got out and went over and sat under a tree, stayed there all day, just sat out there under a tree. Well, late evening some guy who'd just got off work in town went driving on another road across from it. He just happened to glance over there and he saw something. And he thought, "I believe that's a car over there."

So he turned around and went back around and came in behind her. Sure enough, there she sat under a tree. And he said, "What in the world are you doing here?" And she said, "Well, I'm stuck. I've been here for all day."

He said, "Well, let me get you out of here." So he went and got a tractor and they hooked onto her and pulled her out. But Neva wasn't concerned. She's just sitting under that tree all day long. Still, of course, her car hadn't been cleaned even yet. It just sat there caked with mud.

Jay McAlvain, with Choctaw translation by Henry Willis

Anumpa ꝟlhpesa: Conversation

Choctaw, like many American Indian languages, pays special attention to the attitude and tone of speakers in conversation. Choctaw has special forms, often called *discourse markers*, that indicate an attitude or tone that a speaker intends when engaged in conversation. It is often not possible to translate these markers directly; instead we will give examples of situations where the markers are used.

Types of Questions: Using -o, -ha, and cho

We have learned to make yes/no questions using the particle -o at the end of the sentence, like this:

Chimꝟlla yꝟt holisso apisa ia-tuk-o?
Did your child go to school?

We have not yet examined two other question markers, -ha and cho, which are very commonly used to make Choctaw questions. Each gives a different feeling or intention to a question.

Confirmation with -ha

Many times we ask a question to which we already know the answer. We are seeking not information but confirmation from others about an opinion or fact. This is useful in conversation to make small talk. Notice the difference in the intention of the following questions:

a. Lꝟshpah-o?
   Is it hot? (I need to know whether it's hot and don't know already.)
b. Lꝟshpa-ha?
   It's hot, isn't it? (I would like you to agree with me that it's hot.)

(Even though -*ha̱* is actually put together just like *h-o̱*, we will treat it as a single unit, just as we have done with -*hosh* and -*ho̱*, since this is easier to recognize in the written language.)

Polite questions with -*ha̱*

Another use of the -*ha̱* question marker is to ask questions to which an answer is needed, in a somewhat more inviting way. The -*ha̱* marker can be used to indicate the recent past without using *tuk*:

Ish-impa-ha̱?
Have you eaten?

We would not generally say *Ish-impah-o̱?* because this would imply that we are bothering you while you are trying to eat.

When speaking especially politely, we may even dispense with a question marker completely, using *kia* and letting the question trail off:

Ish-impa tuk kia . . .
Did you eat? (Literally, "You ate, but . . .")

This very indirect question is used when you would not want to offend someone by directly requesting information.

Strong questions with *cho*

A third question marker is *cho*. This marker means that the speaker expects an answer, and it is used among friends and same-age family members. It is generally informal in tone and would probably not be used to address an elder or authority figure. *Cho* is used when a conversation is under way and the speakers understand the context:

a. Chi-hohchv̱ffo cho?
   Well, are you hungry? (It's mealtime, and I would like to eat, and expect you to agree.)
b. Ish-impa cho?
   So, did you eat? (I know you left for lunch, and expect you to have eaten.)

Conversational banter with *cho*

Among peers and family, we also use *cho* to lend the sense of the English 'so?', 'well, then', and the like in a teasing or bantering way:

a. Cho! maka-lachi̱-ho̱?
   Am I gonna say that?! *or* So, am I supposed to say that?! *or* Am I supposed to say that, too?!
b. Person A: Chi-bolli-lachi̱!
   Person B: Cho, ma̱!
   Person A: I'll beat you!
   Person B: Bring it on! *or* So, do it!

Discourse Markers

Miha

Another important word used in conversation, and also in story-telling, is *miha*, or *miya*, which means 'say' and especially 'mean'. It can be used in conversation as a way of softening a statement by adding the sense of the English phrase *they say*. In this way, the speaker doesn't have to be perceived as making a claim about something that might not be provable. This is particularly important in Choctaw, and it is used routinely in reporting conversations and telling stories.

a. Chukka apa̱ta yʋt iskʋlli ik-im-iksho, miha.
   The neighbors don't have any money, they say.
b. "Hʋshtula achʋffa mah, nittak ʋt kapʋssa ka̱ oka yʋt kalampit kania...tok miha" (from chapter 22, *Choctaw Language and Culture*).
   It's said that one winter, the day was so cold that the water froze over.
c. "Pokni yʋt afʋmmi pokoli tuklo mʋt tapushik tʋnna i̱punna tok miya" (from chapter 2).
   Grandma was a master weaver at the age of twenty, they say.

Chini

Another discourse expression that is common in Choctaw conversation is *chini*, which is used to comment on something that was not known before. It may be translated a number of ways:

a. Illi tuk<u>a</u> chini.
It seems he died. *or* So, he died! *or* He *did* die. (The person's death was unexpected or not known about beforehand.)
b. Michigan *v*t im-abi tuk<u>a</u> chini!
So, Michigan won!
c. Sapokni *v*t *v*la tuk<u>a</u> chini.
Grandma came, it seems. *or* So, Grandma came!

Chini is used at the end of sentence, joined to the rest of sentence by k<u>a</u> or tuk<u>a</u> as the case may be.

Expressions

Choctaw has a number of conversational expressions that are either not really words or are made up of idiomatic particles. They correspond to English expressions such as *gosh!*; *well, now!* and dozens of others.

Here are some expressions that you may hear conversationally:

omikato	so it is
omishke	Hear! Hear!
inta	Look!
oe	shows impatience or disbelief
h<u>i</u>	shows disgust
ome	all right; indeed
okinta	I dare you!

Other expressions are used to begin sentences in stories or to enter conversations. These expressions correspond to the English *well*; *anyway*; *and then*; *so*; and the like. Some of these are:

mihma
micha
yohmi
mihm*v*t
y*v*mmak<u>i</u>
atukkia

Other expressions are used to signal agreement with a speaker or to emphasize a point in a story. These correspond to the English *surely*; *of course*; and *without a doubt*:

a̲lhi
mv̲lhi
aia̲lhi
yohmi mv̲lhi

ANUMPA

Nouns

himonasi	[hi-mó-nv-si]	minute
nana hokano	[na-na-hó-kv-no]	some thing or another
nashali	[na-shá-li]	car
nanishthalv̲lli	[nan-isht-hv-l'v́l-li]	tractor
ulbal abohli	[ul-bal-a-bóh-li]	backwoods
ulbal	[ul-bal]	the back; the rear

Verbs

akkoa	[ák-kv-wv]	come down; descend
akmo	[ak-mu]	harden; congeal; stiffen
hoppi, hohpi	[hop-pi]	bury a dead creature
nutakachi	[nu-tá-kv-chi]	put beneath; place under
okakania	[o-kv-kv-ni-yv]	sink; drown; become mired
ompohomo, umpohomo	[om-pu-ho-mu]	cover up or bury a thing
opia	[o-pi-yv]	become evening; get dark
tabokoli, tabokuli	[ta-bo-ku-li]	be noon
takali	[ta-ka-li]	hang; be in a position
takalichi	[tv-ká-li-chi]	hang or suspend something

Adjectives

akmo	[ak-mu]	hardened; congealed
ompoholmo, umpoholmo	[om-pu-hol-mu]	covered in or with
takali	[ta-ká-li]	hung up; stuck; hooked

Location Words

| apata | [*v*-pa-t*v*] | on the side of; along the side of |
| ulbal | [ul-bal] | behind; in the rear |

Adverbs

kesha, kisha	[ké-sh*v*]	not yet; not even yet
shohbi	[shoh-bi]	all day; the day up until the evening
shoyohbi	[shó-yoh-bi]	all day long; all the livelong day
y*v*mmimma	[y*v*m-mim-m*v*]	that way

Idioms

ak-chi-kuchi-la-hinla	let me get you out
ch*v*nalichit ch*v*nalichit	spin and spin; keep spinning (wheels)
kana kia	someone; anyone
m*v*lhi	doubtless; truly
ma yohmi k*v*t peh yohmi k*v*t	he just happened to . . .
nach*v*fichi'sh aya	go driving
nana ka	whatever; something like that
nana ho kaniohmi	whatever one does
nitak ach*v*ffa keyukm*v*t tuklo mah	a day or two
tabokoli ont ia	afternoon
tombi pisa nana akohmi	what color it is

Discourse Expressions

aialhi ka	[áy-a-lhi-ka]	sure enough; of course
chini	[che-ni]	so! it seems that . . .
mihm*v*t	[mih-m*v*t]	and then; and (same subject)
mihma	[mih-ma]	and then; and
omikato	[o-mí-ka-to]	expression of surprise: well! my goodness!

yvmmaki	[yvm-mv-kí]	so; thus
yohmi atukkia	[yoh-mi-v-túk-ki-yv]	well; anyway
yohmi mvlhi kiyo kia	[yoh-mi-mv-lhi-kí-yo-ki-yv]	still; of course; but of course

ANUMPA ANUKFILLI: Measuring Time, Distance, and Money

In Choctaw there are various idioms for describing quantities of time and distance. Some of these are quite idiomatic, as they are in English.

Hopaki

This adverb can be used to mean 'at some distance'. The idiom for 'from here' is *pa hikia ka*.

a. Pa hikia ka, tvmaha hopaki kvt kowi tuklo.
   From here, the town is two miles away.
b. Holisso apisa yvt aiitatobushi hikia ka, hopaki kvt kowi iklvnna.
   The school is half a mile from the little store. *Or, in another way of saying the same thing:*
c. Holisso apisa yvt aittatobushi ont ia ka kowi iklvnna.
   The school is half a mile from the little store.

Hvshi Kanvlli and Tabokoli

Telling time in Choctaw is done by simply giving the word for 'hour', *hvshi kanvlli*, and a numeral. The word for 'minute' is *himonasi*. To give both hour and minute, we give the minutes and then the hour, followed by *ontia* 'past'.

a. hvshi kanvlli tuchena
   three o'clock
b. himonasi tuklo
   two minutes
c. himonasi pokoli tuklo, hvshi kanvlli ushta ontia
   twenty minutes past four
d. himonasi talhapi, hvshi kanvlli ontuchena ontia
   five minutes past eight

It is more complicated to talk about general times of day, such as 'noon', *tabokoli,* also spelled *tabokuli.* This word is a verb that refers to the sun's position at the zenith of the sky. 'Afternoon' is *tabokoli ont ia, tabokoli foka* is 'about noon', and *tabokoli fokali* is 'around noon':

a. Tabokolih ma̱ il-impa tuk.
   When it was noon, we ate.
b. Tabokoli ont iah ma̱ pi̱kanomi tuklo kʋt pi̱-pisat itʋlachi tuk.
   In the afternoon two of our relatives came to see us.
c. Allo̱si yʋt tabokoli fokali nusit ia tuk.
   The baby went to sleep around noon.

Tʋli Holisso and *Sint*

The Choctaw word for 'dollar' is *tʋli holisso* (literally 'coin paper'. *Tʋli* is of course the word for metal, and its meaning was extended to refer to a coin of precious metal. It is perhaps amusing to think that the Choctaw expression also means 'metal paper'.) *Sint* is borrowed directly from the English word 'cent'.

tʋli holisso talhapi	five dollars
tʋli holisso talhapi pokoli	fifty dollars
tʋli holisso ontuchena sint pokkoli aiena	eight dollars and ten cents
tʋli holisso achʋffa sint pokoli ontuklo aiena	one dollar and seventy cents

Abʋchi

Chi-anukfo̱kah-o̱?

Have a Choctaw conversation with someone, using some of the discourse and conversation markers introduced in this chapter.

Anumpa ʋlhpesa

A. What is the difference in the meanings and intentions of these sentences? When might you use each of them?

1. Aiitatoba iah chi-bvnnah-o̱?
2. Aittatoba iah chi-bvnna-ha̱?
3. Aittatoba iah chi-bvnna cho?

B. Give the Choctaw for each of the following. There is more than one correct way to do so.

1. John was the last boy to come into the room.
2. I went to the shoe store first, then I went to buy groceries.
3. Sunday will be my last day.
4. This is the baby's first tooth.
5. Mother prepared the meat beforehand.

Holissochi

Write a short story or essay on a topic of your choice. In it include at least two conversation or discourse markers and at least one idiom. Translate to Nahullo Anumpa.

CHAPTER 4

Aiisht Ahollo 'The Miracle'

**Choctaw Text and Translation: *Aiisht Ahollo* 'The Miracle',
by Bill Nowlin**

*Choctaw folklorist Tim Tingle tells us that one of the important kinds
of narrative among modern Choctaw people is the "miracle story." The
miracle is most often about deliverance from certain death or fatal illness,
or an unexplainable cure, as in this story told to Mr. Tingle by Bill Nowlin
about his uncle, Hank Brown. Moshi Hank was a sailor in World War II
who was cured of hopelessly grave wounds by his Choctaw grandmother
using traditional medicine. The Choctaw translation is by Henry Willis.*

Yakni Moma Tvnvp Atukla isht vshwanchi moma ka amoshi, Hank
Hatonlakna yvt tanampi oka peni chito imisht asha, im-isht vtta tok.
Aiitibi aiklvnanchit maya ma, ibbak afabik imma yvt peni itanampo chito
isht bakli tiwa ya, peni isht vtta achvffa kvt, akvmmit isht issot litolit aivlhichi tok. Tvshka imomvchi abeka aiasha chukka bilika moma ishahli,
Houston, Tixas, peni chito fohkit falammint pila tok. Ibbak vt lhilahli
kania atoko alikchi yvt bvsht tvblachi hosh oklah im-anukfila tok.

Oka Peni Ishtasha yvt nan ahnit kaniohmichi kvt ishki ya, Ishki Willat,
ilauet pisat ishtia tok. Yukpalachi im-anukfila hosh ia, kia Ishki Willat ato
imanukfilat inla ahni hosh aya tok. Chahta iklvnna yvt atok mikmvt hvshi
yvmmak fokali ka ikhish ilapit ikbi yo aiasanochi atok. Moshi Hank ya
kana't apesachi keyu takla ma Ishki Willat nafohkachit tahli mvt, apelat

38

abeka aiasha akuhchit ichukka ishtia tok. Oshitek ʋt imoshi ibabinilit anta na iyup ʋt Tixas Hʋshi Akuchaka tiak iti foka ikhish albo aiowachi ho ishtia tok. Ichukka falamat ʋlah mʋt ikhish lawa kanihmi ikbi cha ibbak ahʋm-michi na nitak ninak kaniohmi foka tok.

Peni Ishtʋtta alikchi yʋt kania tuka oklah akostininchih mʋt Oka Alaka Apesachi, isht ilawiha, isht onnuchit yukachit aboha kʋllo fokih bʋnna tok. Nuktanla hosh okhisa ont afamat ipoknakni yʋt himmona kia atoksali kanimma kia issa chatuk keyu ka im-anoli tok, micha yʋmmʋt ibbak achʋffa illa kʋt Nasis itibachi kʋt ik-ahobo ketok.

Achi tok miha, "Lakoffichit tahli-lik mʋt falamichit pit chi-chʋffichi-lachi. Itibi ahinlak mʋt, ashakapat alhipullik ma ibbak toklo ishi moma ahinla."

Oklah pafachi kʋt ik-anukfilo tuk: hʋshi kaniohmit taha ma, ibbak isht abeka yʋt haiaka keyu taha mah, Peni Ishtʋtta alikchi yʋt falamat isht toksalahinlat taha ka im-anoa tok. Peni Ishtʋtta akinli ibafoka na nitak imalhpisa alhipulli tok mikmʋt Tʋli Hullo Chokash Hummaiyi Inunchi anoti Kuchi Holitopa ima tok. Himakma ohoyo ilap ahni lhamko hosh ishahlichi fehna tok.

During World War II, my mother's brother, Hank Brown, was serving on a battleship in the U.S. Navy. In the heat of battle, his left hand was crushed when the breach block of one of the ship's big guns was slammed on it by another sailor. He was shipped back to the veterans' hospital closest to his home, which was in Houston, Texas. His hand was so badly mangled that the doctors decided to cut it off.

When the navy notified his mother of the decision, she took her mother, Ma Willard, to see him. Her hope was to cheer him up, but Ma Willard had a different plan. She was half Choctaw Indian and she had been raised in a time and place where the only medicine was homemade. Uncle Hank was not under guard, so Ma Willard got him dressed and the two women ushered him out of the hospital and took him to her house. She left her daughter to sit with Hank and she had her son-in-law drive her into the piney woods of east Texas to gather medicinal plants. She returned home and made a series of poultices that she kept applied to Hank's hand day and night for days.

When the navy doctors found Hank gone, they sent the Shore Patrol to arrest him for desertion. Ma Willard met them at the door and calmly informed them that no grandson of hers ever deserted from any "job-of-work" and that he would be useless to fight the Nazis with one hand. She said, "When I get him healed up, I'll send'm back to ya. He'll be fit to fight, and he will still have both hands when this fuss is over."

They decided not to challenge her. Some time later, he recovered enough use of his hand—with no signs of infection—that the doctors pronounced him fit to return to service. He stayed in the navy for the duration and was given a Purple Heart and an honorable discharge. Another strong-willed woman prevailed.

Bill Nowlin, with Choctaw translation by Henry Willis

ANUMPA ꝞLHPESA: Ways to Say *Or*

Contrast

Although it seems easy, distinguishing between two or more things or situations can be one of the most difficult tasks in many languages. We have seen that Choctaw uses special markers to show contrast (see also chapter 11 in this volume and chapter 24 in *Choctaw Language and Culture*). There are other ways to show the kind of contrast expressed by the English word *or*.

Disjunction: *Or*

The technical term for the idea expressed by *or* is *disjunction*: it is the opposite of **conjunction**. Conjunction, expressed in English most commonly by the word *and*, puts together things and ideas, while disjunction sets out a group of things and ideas and then selects one of them, in contrast to the others. So, in English we have:

Do want coffee, tea, or lemonade?
Is that cat playing with a mouse or chewing on my shoe?
Come back with my homework or else I will make you wish you had!
We will either visit our relatives in Atoka or buy Grandma a ticket to visit us.

Notice that in all of these sentences the speaker puts forth a set of choices, both (or all) of which cannot happen or be true at the same time.

In Choctaw, just as there are many ways to express conjunction, there are many ways to express the idea of *or*. Some of these are the words *chomba*, *keyukmvt / keyukma*, *amba*, and *kanimampo*.

Chomba

One fairly simple way to express 'or' is with *chomba*. This word is used when we are distinguishing situations. It appears between the two ideas, expressed in predicates, that are being contrasted.

    a. Ofi vt chito yo chomba ossi yo?
       Is the dog big or little? (Literally, "Is the dog a big one or a little one?")
    b. Oka yvt lvchah-o chomba kapvssah-o?
       Is the water hot or cold?

Keyukmvt/Keyukma

A more general way to express 'or' is with *keyukmvt* and its non-subject form *keyukma*. Using this pair is the common way to distinguish nouns and has the sense of the English phrase *if not, then*.

    a. Ofi keyukmvt katos vt nipi vpachi.
       The dog or the cat will eat the meat. (Literally, "The dog—if not, then the cat—will eat the meat.")
    b. "Atoko afvmmi ontuklo keyukmvt ontuchina siah ma, hapichukka atokla kvt toba tok" (from chapter 1).
       Then, when I was seven or eight years old, our second home was built. (The numbers refer to the subject *siah*: When I was seven or I was eight years . . .)
    c. Hattakshali keyukma peni chompa-lachi.
       I'll buy a car or a boat.

This is also a common way to contrast clauses. Note that we change form depending on whether the subjects of the clauses are the same or different.

    a. Onnakma Hvshki vt ilhpak chompachi keyukmvt ikanomi pisat ayachi.
       Tomorrow Mother will buy groceries or she'll visit relatives.
    b. Ofi vt nipi vpachi keyukma katos vt vpachi.
       The dog will eat the meat or the cat will eat it.
    c. "Ninak lawa ho svshki vt ninak iklvnna keyukmvt hvshi kanvlli tuklo keyukmvt tuchena tani cha . . ." (from chapter 2).

Many nights my mother rose in the middle of the night or two o'clock or three o'clock and . . .

d. "Tikba nittak achvffa keyukmvt tuklo mah, nana ka̲, omba tok . . ." (from chapter 3).
A day or two before, something like that, it had rained . . .

Amba

Yet another way to choose between alternatives is with *amba*, which we can often translate with the English phrase *either–or*. *Amba* has only one form.

a. Ish-iachi̲h-o̲ amba ilvppa ish-antachi̲h-o̲?
Will you go or will you stay here?
b. A̲kana Akansa asha ka̲ pisat a̲ya-lachi̲ amba Iti Tanampo Kobafa atoksalit isht ia-lachi̲.
I will either visit my friends in Arkansas or I will start working in Broken Bow.

Kanimampo

When choosing between precisely two things, we can emphasize this by using *kanimampo*. Notice that the two choices appear together, followed by *kanimampo*. Either *kvt* or *ka̲* is used to set off the phrase. *Either–or* is a good English translation.

a. Chan Bil kanimampo kvt chukka pa̲ chompachi̲.
Either John or Bill will buy this house.
b. Sapokni chipokni kanimampo ka̲ pvska champuli pa̲ ima-lachi̲.
I'll give this sweet bread to either my grandma or your grandma.
c. Allo̲si vt pishokchi takkon okchi kanimampo ka̲ ishkoh bvnna.
The baby wants to drink either milk or apple juice.

ANUMPA

Nouns

abeka aiasha chukka	[v-be-kv-áy-a-shv-chúk-kv]	hospital
aiisht ahollo	[ay-isht-v-hól-lu]	miracle

aiitibi	[ay-i-tí-bi]	battle; fight
alaka	[ʋ-lá-ka]	edge; border
albo	[ál-bu]	forest under growth
ibbak afabik imma	[ib-bak a-fa-bik ím-mʋ]	left hand
imisht asha	[i-misht á-shʋ]	the (military) service
isht bakli tiwa	[isht bak-li tí-wʋ]	breach block
iyup	[í-yup]	son-in-law
oka alaka	[o-kʋ ʋ-lá-kʋ]	shore
Oka Peni Ishtasha	[o-kʋ pe-ni isht-á-shʋ]	the navy
peni isht ʋtta	[pe-ni isht ʋt-tʋ]	sailor
shakapa	[shʋ-ká-pʋ]	turmoil; uproar
tʋshka imomʋchi	[tʋsh-kʋ i-mó-mʋ-chi]	veteran
tanampi	[ta-ná-pi]	war; hostility
tiak	[tí-ak]	pine; pinewood

Verbs

akostininchi	[ʋ-kos-ti-ni̱-chi]	find out; discover
ahʋmmichi	[a-hʋm-mi-chi]	anoint or rub another person
ʋshwanchi	[ʋsh-wa̱-chi]	be engaged; be going on
bʋsht tʋbli	[bʋsht tʋb-li]	amputate; cut off
chʋffichi	[chʋf-fi-chi]	send off
im-isht ʋtta	[im-isht ʋt-tʋ]	be in service; be occupied (Gp. 3)
aiʋlhichi	[ai-ʋ-lhi-chi]	terminate; bring to an end
aiiklʋnachi	[ai-ik-lʋ-na-chi]	put in the middle of
bakli	[bak-li]	split something into large pieces
litoli	[li-to-li]	crush; smash
talaia	[tʋ-lai-yʋ]	be set; be placed somewhere
talali	[tʋ-la-li]	set in place; put somewhere
taloha	[ta-lo-hʋ]	be set somewhere (plural things)
talohli	[ta-loh-li]	set plural things in place
talohmaya	[ta-loh-ma-yʋ]	stand around (plural)

Adjectives

| imomʋchi | [i-mó-mʋ-chi] | old; experienced |
| kanihmi | [ka-níh-mi] | healing; convalescing |

| lhilahli | [lhi-láh-li] | mangled; torn in many places |
| toklo | [tok-lu] | both |

Idioms

ashakapat alhipullik ma	when the fuss is over
ilap ahni lhamko	strong-willed
ilapit ikbi	make by oneself; homemade
isht onnuchi	take by lawful force
nan ahnit kaniohmachi kvt	decision (*Or* whatever was in their mind to do)
nitak ninak kaniohmi foka	day and night (*Or* through that time)
tanampi oka peni chito	battleship
Yakni Moma Tvnvp Atukla	World War II

ANUMPA ANUKFILLI: *Talaia* and Its Variations

We know that Choctaw has a great many verbs that refer specifically to location and position, and that Choctaw verbs often incorporate singular and plural subjects and objects into their meanings. One useful group of such verbs is *talaia* 'be set, placed, or situated' and its variations.

Talaia

This general word means 'be set' and is used to indicate that something not alive is situated somewhere. It takes a singular subject. This is contrasted with *hikia*, which refers specifically to the vertical direction of something that stands.

a. Chukka makosh nvnih tuklo itatakla talaia.
   That house was situated between two hills.
b. Ishtishko vt aiimpushi otalaia.
   A glass was placed on a little table.
c. Ohoyo mvt issuba kostini ka otalaiah beka.
   That woman frequently rides a horse that's gentle.

Otalaia means 'placed on' and can also mean 'ride'.

Talali

The transitive member of this set (a transitive verb has both a subject and an object), now with a singular object, means *place or set something*:

Ishtishko ya aiimpushi ma ish-talali ka ikhana-li.
I know that you put the glass on that little table.

Taloha
When plural things are placed or situated, we use *taloha*:

Hattakshali lʋwa hosh kashak ashaka taloha.
There are a lot of cars (situated) behind the barn.

Talohli
The transitive member with plural objects means *place or set plural things:*.

Aki ʋt chukka bilika iti lumbo talohli tuk.
Dad placed the logs near the house.

Talohmaya
This variation, compounded with *maya*, is used with living things and means 'stand around':

Himmithoa kanohmi hosh holisso apisa talohmaya.
Several young people are standing around the school.

ABʋCHI

Chi-anukfokah-o?

Examine all the vocabulary words relating to war and show how their meanings are made up of other Choctaw words and markers.

Anumpa ʋlhpesa

A. Make these sentences in Choctaw. There is more than one correct way to do so.

1. We will plant cantaloupe or watermelon.
2. The chief will either write a letter or go to bed.
3. You or I will do the laundry.
4. Are the sailors young or experienced?

B. What do these sentences mean?

1. Chiyup keyukma chippochi pisat ish-ayah-o?
2. Nitak ninak kanohmi foka ma tvshka moma kvt itibi tok.
3. Peni ishtvtta akosh tiak peni toklo litoli tuk.

C. Using all of the ways to say *or* in Choctaw, write two sentences exemplifying each.

Holissochi

Write a story or essay of at least ten sentences and using at least five new vocabulary words. Include at least one instance of disjunction (*or*) in your work. Translate to natural English.

CHAPTER 5

"*Chimilhfiopak*"
'Your Life' and "*Aiena E-taloa*"
'We Sing Together'

Choctaw Text and Translation: "Chimilhfiopak" 'Your Life', by Henry Willis, and "Aiena E-taloa" 'We Sing Together', by Phillip Carroll Morgan

These are some of the first poems to appear in the Choctaw language (the very first known poem, written in 1878, appears in chapter 11). The first, "Chimilhfiopak," was written by Henry Willis in memory of his sister, Rebecca Harris, and recited at her funeral. It has been borrowed by other Choctaw people, who have heard it and wanted to similarly honor their loved ones. The author began writing Choctaw poetry at about age eleven while attending Goodland Academy, one of the Indian boarding schools, near Hugo, Oklahoma. He says the metaphor for this poem came from a story told in a Sunday school class, when Jesus was said to comment on the forget-me-not, whose bloom lasts only one day.

Yakni apaknaka ilᵥppa ish'la kᵥt,
chimilhfiopak ᵥt,
hᵥshi akuchaka imma hᵥshi ᵥt awakaiya ak̲o̲ chiyuhmi tok.

Micha yakni apaknaka ish-noh̲o̲wa moyyoma k̲a̲,
chimilhfiopak ᵥt
lhamko mikmᵥt shohpakali achukma kᵥt,
hᵥshi ᵥt ont tabokoli ak̲o̲ chiyyohmi tok.

Himak a͟ Hv̓shi v̓t okv̓tolat maha͟ya ka͟ e-chibanoho͟wa tok,
himak v̓la kia il-anowat a͟ya atukv̓t ont aiv̓lhit maha͟ya.
Ilv̓ppa͟ hikiat ia hokano
chishno akbano hosh ish-noho͟wa makachi͟ pulla.

Yohmi kia ish-onak ma,
la͟wa kv̓t chi-afv̓mmachi͟,
micha na
yukpa hosh chi-ayukpachi afehna achi͟ hoke.

You came upon this earth,
your life,
like the sun rising in the east.

And while you were walking upon this earth
your life
was strong and bright
as the midday sun.

Until now we have walked with you as the sun has moved west,
however, we are coming to a journey's end.
From here on
you shall ever walk alone.

However, when you reach there,
many will meet you,
and
with gladness they will welcome you well.

Henry Willis, with English translation by
Carole Willis and Juliane Willis Judd

The second poem, "Aiena E-taloa," is by the Choctaw-Chickasaw poet *Phillip Carroll Morgan*, who began to study the Choctaw language as an adult at the University of Oklahoma and wished to express his thoughts in the language of his ancestors. This is one of several Choctaw language poems that Mr. Morgan has written.

hushi ossi lusah micha tohbi ʋt
iti hahe chaha binilih
hohchʋffo

illimpa atahli-li
onish micha ṯachi kʋlloh
himak ʋpachi̱
hushi moma kʋt ʋpachi

bokushi e-heli
oka kapʋssa il-ishko
hattak il-i̱-taloa
hattak ʋt pi̱-taloa

small black and white bird
sitting in the tall bare acorn tree
is hungry

i am preparing corn
millet and hard corn
then he will eat
all the birds will eat

we fly to the creek
we drink the cold water
we sing to the man
the man sings to us

Phillip Carroll Morgan (Originally published in The Fork-in-the-Road
Indian Poetry Store, *by Phillip Carroll Morgan (Cambridge: Salt
Publishing, 2006). Reprinted by permission of the publisher.)*

ANUMPA ʋLHPESA: Emphatic Modifiers and the Optative Mood: *Illa, Bano,* and *Beka*

There are many ways that language can make something more
prominent. We can raise the pitch or volume of our voices, or put words
in a different order, or use special words whose job is to point out some
expression. One very important system of this kind in Choctaw is the large

set of definiteness markers (see chapter 10). Another strategy is to use adverbs to modify some idea or object. We have already been introduced to some of these in the texts. Among the commonest of these adverbs are *illa* and *bano*, both of which mean 'only; alone'. *Bano* can also be used to express the optative mood, which could be translated as 'if only . . .'

Illa

This adverb may be used with both noun phrases and verb phrases to express the sense of 'only' in English. In the noun phrase, it refers to something singular, as in the English phrase *the only one*. In the noun phrase, *illa* appears in the last position for modifiers, after the noun and any other modifiers, in the reverse order of English.

  a. "Chukka itabana, aboha achvffa illa yo . . ." (from chapter 1).
     A log house, only one room . . .
  b. "Sa-hofantit vtta-lih ma, Chahta Anumpa mak illa ho chukka asha
     yvt okla itimanumpuli bieka tok" (from chapter 2).
     When I was growing up, the household used to speak only Choctaw.
     or When I was growing up, the only thing the household used to
     speak was Choctaw.

Frequently we use the definite particle *mak* to form *mak illa*, which may be translated 'the only thing' or 'it only'.

Just as in English, we may move *illa* to the predicate to change the focus of the sentence. Notice the slight difference in meaning in the following examples:

  a. Aki illa pisa-li tuk.
     I saw only my father.
  b. Aki pisa-li illa tuk.
     I only saw my father.

When we use *illa* in the predicate, it must appear after the verb and before the tense marker (it is one of the aspectual adverbs rather than a manner adverb).

Illa can also be used to mean 'alone' in the sense of 'by itself.' We use the subject marker *hosh* rather than *yvt* when a phrase with *illa* appears as the subject of a sentence. Try to understand the difference between examples above and example a. below.

a. A̱ki illa hosh hiki̱a.
My father is standing alone.
b. A̱ki ʋt hiki̱ah illa.
My father is only standing.

Bano

Another word that is similar but not identical to *illa* is *bano*. This word implies that something is separated from a group, pointing out that it is alone. Like subjects that use *illa*, subjects with *bano* take the *hosh* subject marker. *Bano* may refer to plural things that are singled out in a group.

a. A̱ki bano hosh hiki̱a.
My father alone is standing. (May be translated 'My father is standing alone.')

The sentences "A̱ki illa hosh hiki̱a" and "A̱ki bano hosh hiki̱a" are generally interchangeable, but the latter implies that there is a group of people among whom my father is the sole person standing. The former does not imply that my father is distinct in any way.

a. Wak bano hosh hiki̱a.
˙ Only a cow is standing there.
b. Wak bano hosh hiohma̱ya.
Only cows are standing there.

We often use the word for 'self', *ilap*, to emphasize the solitary sense in the English phrase 'by oneself'. Person markers are attached to *ilap*, never to *bano* (or *illa*). Similarly, *mak bano* is used as a general third-person pronoun since we don't use *bano* by itself:

sa'lap bano; sa'lap illa (sa + ilap)	by myself
ilap bano; ilap illa	by himself/herself
chi'lap bano; chi'lap illa	by yourself
pi'lap bano; pi'lap illa	by ourselves
hachi'lap bano; hachi'lap illa	by yourselves

We may attach the definite particle *ak* to both *illa* and *bano* to form the emphatic definites *akilla* and *akbano*. These may be translated as the emphatic 'oneself', as in 'he himself'.

   a. Chishno akbano hosh nowat ish-aya makachi̱ pulla.
      You shall walk alone. (You yourself shall walk alone.)
   b. ʋno akbano hosh Missippi ahanta-li.
      I myself live in Mississippi.
   c. Pishno akilla pi-apelah bʋnna.
      He wants to help us alone.

Bano in the verb phrase

When *bano* appears in the verb phrase, it becomes an aspectual adverb and takes the form *hebano*. Now it has the meaning of 'surely can' or 'surely does' in the emphatic sense.

Hattak mʋt balili hebano.
That man sure can run. (*Not* "That man only runs.")

Bato and *bat*

There is a second form of *bano*, namely, *bato*, which has some old differences in usage that have fallen together in modern times:

   a. Mak bato hosh nowat a̱ya.
      He's walking alone.
   b. Ilap bato hosh to̱ksali tuk.
      He worked alone.
   c. Wak bato ho̱ pi̱sa-li.
      I saw only the cows.

The contraction of *bano hosh* or of *bato hosh* produces *bat*. When we use *bat*, we omit *hosh*, since it's built in:

Mak bat a̱ya.
He's alone.

Multiplication

Bat is also the word used to express multiplication problems:

   a. Pokkoli bat pokkoli ʋt talhepa achʋffa toba.
      Ten times ten is one hundred.
   b. Hʋnnali bat achʋffa ʋt hʋnnali toba.
      Six times one is six.

Beka

We have studied *beka* and its intensive form *bieka* as aspectual adverbs, meaning they have the sense of the English 'often, usually, frequently, all the time' (see chapter 17 in *Choctaw Language and Culture*). When *beka* appears in the noun phrase, that is, when it modifies a noun, it has a very different meaning. (It is like *moma, pulla, puta*, and *ma*, which change their meanings depending on where they appear.) In the noun phrase, *beka* means 'only' or 'alone', and like *bano*, it implies picking something out from a group. Like *illa* and *bano*, subjects take the *hosh* subject marker.

a. Ilap beka hosh mitachi.
   He'll be coming by himself.
b. Sa'lap beka hosh ona-li tuk.
   I arrived alone.

Remember that, as in the following examples, *beka* in the predicate is an aspectual adverb, meaning 'usually':

a. Hattak bano hosh ilvppa binilih beka.
   Only the man usually sits here.
b. Chi'lap beka hosh impah beka.
   You usually dine by yourself. (This example contains both uses of *beka*.)

In usage, most Choctaw speakers freely use all three of these forms, which are for the most part synonymous:

Ilap beka hosh . . . *or* Ilap bano hosh . . . *or* Ilap illa hosh . . . mitachi.
He'll be coming by himself.

The Optative Mood

The term *optative mood* is used to describe the expression of what one would desire or hope for. The following examples are English expressions of the optative mood:

If only Christmas would come!
Lord help him!

May your days be filled with joy.
Would that my grades improved! (This is a bit old-fashioned.)

We can use *bano* to express this mood in Choctaw. To do so, we attach the *-k* marker to the verb, followed by *bano* (remember that the desired state has not actually happened yet, so Choctaw requires the "hypothetical" or "if" marker).

In addition, the pitch of the voice must rise on the verb and drop on *bano* (similar to how Choctaw yes/no questions are formed).

   a. Mịtit ʋlak bano!
     If only he'd come!
   b. Hokbano!
     If only!

ANUMPA

Nouns

aboha aialhtoka	[a-bo-hʋ ai-ʋlh-tó-kʋ]	office
aiʋlhi	[ai-ʋ-lhi]	end
anumpa atatoa	[a-nọ-pʋ a-tʋ-tó-wʋ]	poem
haiyokpulo okchaki	[hai-yok-pu-lo ok-chá̲-ki]	salad; greens
holba toba	[hol-bʋ tó-bʋ]	picture
ilhfiopak	[ilh-fi-ó-pʋk]	life (of a person)
ishttoksali	isht-tọ́k-sʋ-li]	machine; tool
iskʋlli apota	[is-kʋl-li a-pó-tʋ]	bank (financial)
mʋlahtushi	[mʋ-láh-tu-shi]	electricity
nihi lʋwa	[ni-hi lʋ-wʋ]	tomato (and other seeded fruits)
nipi patoa	[ni-pi pʋ-tó-ʋ]	ground meat
olhti	[ólh-ti]	government
poa alhpoa	[po-ʋ alh-pó-ʋ]	pet

Verbs

aiʋlhi	[ai-ʋ-lhi]	end at
ahinna	[a-hin-nʋ]	care for or accompany someone
bʋska	[bʋs-kʋ]	gamble; bet

ilatomba	[i-la-to̱-bʋ]	save
chahikli	[cha-hik-li]	limp (walk)
kinakli	[ki-nak-li]	move sporadically; stumble
makachi̱	[ma-ka-chi̱]	it shall be
shohpakali	[shoh-pʋ-ka-li]	shine

Adjectives

imalheka	[i-ma-lhé-kʋ]	unfortunate
imalhekahinla	[i-ma-lhe-kʋ-hi̱-lʋ]	unsafe
imalhekahekeyu	[i-ma-lhe-kʋ-hé-ki-yu]	safe (*Or* not unsafe)

Idioms

| aivlhit mahaya (plural suject) | are coming to an end |
| pʋla mʋlahtushi shapoa | lamp |

ANUMPA ANUKFILLI: *Takali* 'Hanging Around'

Takali

Takali is one of the verbs of position, and has a large number of meanings that seem unrelated unless one realizes that the basic meaning of *takali* is 'placed in a position.' Because English so often uses the verb 'be' to express location, *takali* is often simply translated with a form of 'be'.

A second meaning for *takali* is 'hang' (which is of course a position). As a verb of position, *takali* appears frequently with modifying forms, especially -*t* forms, to complete its meaning.

    a. Himakano, chukfi lhioli hosh takali.
       Presently, he's chasing a rabbit.
    b. Ohoyo ʋt nowat takali.
       The woman is beginning to walk.
    c. Osapa mʋt takali.
       The field is there.

In example a. above, the literal meaning is something close to "He is in a position of chasing a rabbit." In b., *takali* tells us that the woman is in a position, and *nowat* tells us that the kind of movement that she will do is walking. In c., *takali* has its simplest meaning, of being in a position.

Takali is also used for 'hang'. With the causative marker *-chi*, it means to 'hang something':

Holba toba ∨ba takalichi.
He hung up the picture.

The stative form of *tak̲ali* means 'hung'. *O̲tak̲ali* means 'be hung on something':

Aboha holita o̲tak̲ali.
It's hung on the wall.

In a related word, *takak̲ali* means 'to circle':

Hushi m∨t takak̲alit hika.
The bird is flying in circles.

Hanging Around

There are many Choctaw expressions that express being in or leaving a place, either with someone or alone. The vast majority of these expression are made with the *-t* form plus the verb *a̲ya*, or *m̲aya* for plural verbs.

ahinnat a̲ya	accompany someone
aienat a̲ya	go along with someone
akkia a̲ya	go too
ibataklat a̲ya	hang out with someone
ibach∨ffat a̲ya	run away with someone
talohma̲ya	stand around, plural
∨ttat a̲ya	hang out; hang around
takalit a̲ya	hang out; hang around
takohlit m̲aya	hang around, plural

AB∨CHI

Chi-anukf̲okah-o̲?

Translate again Mr. Willis's poem, using your own words. Which do you prefer: a close match to the meaning, or a poetic flow to the English words? It is hard to do both!

Examine Mr. Morgan's poem. How did he use his knowledge of the Choctaw language to make poetry? How is his style different from Mr. Willis's?

Anumpa *v*lhpesa

A. Write five sentences using *illa*, making sure you use all of the usages of this word. Translate to English.

B. Write five sentences using a form of *bano* and making sure you use all usages, including the optative mood. Translate to English.

C. Translate these multiplication problems to Choctaw:

1. Six times three is eighteen.
2. One hundred times ten is one thousand.
3. Four times seven is twenty-eight.
4. Eight times ten is eighty.
5. Twelve times twelve is one hundred forty-four

D. What do these sentences mean?

1. Nihi l*v*wa illa hosh aiimpa talaia.
2. Anumpa atatoa holissochi-lik bano!
3. Chi'lap bano hosh *v*ttat ish-a̱ya ha̱?

E. Use *beka* in both its usages: write two sentences with *beka* in the noun phrase and two with it in the predicate. Translate to English, paying close attention to the difference in meaning.

Holissochi

Write a poem in Choctaw. You do *not* need to translate it to English.

CHAPTER 6

Hokni Nefa Imapolusli Himona 'Aunt Neva's New Tires'

Choctaw Text and Translation: *Hokni Nefa Imapolusli Himona* 'Aunt Neva's New Tires', by Tim Tingle

Aunt Neva, who was introduced in chapter 3, has become something of a folk legend, according to Choctaw folklorist Tim Tingle, who has recorded the oral history of many Choctaw people in both Oklahoma and Mississippi. Here is one of the stories that he has heard told about Aunt Neva's driving habits.

Hattakshali ya, ahokni Nefa yvt ivlli isht ayopomachi kvt isht im-alheka beka tok; yohmi kia hattakshali isht chanvlli apolusli vt pih momat tahat kania atoko, polaka himmona yo chompat abihlit tahli tok. Pikana pisat il-ilhkoli hosh, hattakshali isht ayat hina pvtha il-itanowa tok; mak fokali ma shali okhisushi lhipullichit pit e-pisah ma, chanvlli yvt hina chanvllit aya tok. Shanaioa hosh pihina ikpvtho pit chukoah mvt misha mahaiya tok. Ant pi maiya fehnah ma, chanvlli apolusli a lapalika tohbi himmona yo pisa-li tok.

"Pokni, chanvlli apolusli lapalika tohbi himmona pih himo ish-chompa tuk keyoh-o?" im-achi-li tok.

Ome atokia, Hokni yvt pvlhkichi alhi hosh isht ayah mvt chvnaha tuchina ho chanvllichit isht ayahinla chatuk, okla achvffa't achih billia atok. Atoko ont aialhi tok, Hokni vt hattakshali ont svllahachih ma, ashaka vlhi yvt akkitolat tvli pvtha isso mah, kanima moma luak polohli-chit pila tok. Folotat hina apotaka pit e-hilechih mvt itayokomat kania hosh e-kuchawihat ulbal pila chanaha apolusli lhioli hosh oklah e-tʋkohlit maya tok.

It just pained Aunt Neva to no end to have to spend money on that car, but the tires were just shot and she finally bought new ones. We were driving to see some friends, going down the highway, when we looked out the window and a tire was rolling down the road. It swerved over in the lane in front of us and kept on rolling. When it passed us I saw it was a new whitewall tire.

"Aunt Neva," I said, "didn't you just buy whitewalls?"

Well, everybody always said Aunt Neva drove so fast, she could drive on three wheels. And, sure enough, when she slowed down, Aunt Neva's rear end hit the pavement, sending sparks flying everywhere. We pulled over, scrambled out, and chased that tire down the road.

Tim Tingle, with Choctaw translation by Henry Willis

Anumpa ʋlhpesa: Negative Conditionals and Comparisons: *Unless, Except, and Yet*

One of the most complicated ideas in human speech is negation, as simple as it might seem. We have learned how to make straightforward negative statements with *kiyo* and the *ik-o* set of markers; we have learned the negative mood markers such as *ahekeyu*, and we have learned about the complicated notions of *or* and *but*. Following that path, we now turn to the notions of *unless, except*, and *yet*.

Negative Conditionals

The English word *unless* seems to be included in a positive state-ment, but it means "something will happen if something else doesn't happen." So, "The landlord will evict me unless I pay the rent," really means "The landlord will evict me *if I don't* pay the rent."

In the Choctaw expressions for this idea, both the *if* and the *not* appear. There is more than one way to do so.

Notice that we always use a future marker in the first clause, the one where we are promising or threatening something, because it always has to do with something that has not actually happened. The *if* marker takes care of the second clause.

Kiyo ahokma

One way to express the *if . . . not* or *unless* idea is with the expression *kiyo ahokma*. This expression appears at the end of the clause:

    a. Allo̲si *v*t yaiyachi̲ ish-ipeta kiyo ahokma.
        The baby will cry unless you feed him.
    b. Ia-lachi̲ is-si-apela kiyo ahokma.
        I'll leave unless you help me.

We can make both expressions negative:

    c. Chibanowat ia-lahekeyu ish-salahachi̲ kiyo ahokma.
        I won't travel with you unless you slow down.

ik-o . . . -k ma̲

Another way to achieve this effect is by using the *ik-o* negative markers and finishing the verb with *-k ma̲:*

    a. Holisso apisa ia-lachi̲ ik-ombok ma̲.
        I'll go to school unless it rains.
    b. T*v*maha iachi̲ ik-oktoshok ma̲.
        He'll go to town unless it snows.
    c. H*v*shki *v*t ilaiyukpahekeyu ke-talowok ma̲.
        Mother won't enjoy herself unless we sing.

Negative Comparison

Another very complicated notion is that expressed by the English *except*, which allows us to make a statement about something and then negate that statement for the thing that is "excepted." In Choctaw, we have no comparable word that does this, so the entire idea is expressed fully.

    Moma pi̲sa-li kia a̲ki illakak*o* ak-peso ketuk.
    I saw everyone except my father.

In the example above, the Choctaw literally means, "I saw everyone, but my father alone I didn't see."

    Illa 'alone, by itself' is used to point out the excepted thing, and we often use an emphatic marker such as *ak*o̲ to make the point stronger:

ʋlla moma kʋt itawashoha kia Meli illakato ik-washoho.
All the children are playing together except Mary.

In this example, Meli takes the contrastive subject marker *-ato*, which becomes *-kato* when used with a predicate such as *illa*. This helps to point out that *Meli* is distinct, or an exception. Literally, we say "All of the children are playing together, but Mary alone is not playing."

ketuk

The negative particle *ke* is often combined with the past tense marker *tuk* to make a negative past-tense marker, *ketuk*, which becomes *ketok* in the remote past. This may be used with other negatives in the sentence to strengthen the negation. See chapter 9 for more discussion about this particle. Use the *ik-o* form of the negative.

    a.   Issito keyukma ahe ik-pim-iksho ketuk.
           We didn't have pumpkins or potatoes either.
    b.   Chula yʋt akak moma ka lhioli kia akak nakni illa ik-lhiolo ketuk.
           The fox chased all the chickens except the rooster. (Literally, "The fox chased all the chickens, but the rooster alone it did *not* chase.")

Kesh, Kesha, Kisha: 'Yet'

The word *yet* in English has several meanings, but one of the commonest is the sense of marking time up until the present, with reference to some event that should occur at some point. It very often carries a negative sense: something hasn't happened *yet*. It is best to use one of the English perfect tenses to translate, to give the sense of time traveling from the past to some later point. See chapter 12 for more discussion of compound tenses.

In Choctaw the set of clause conjunctions *kesh, kesha* (sometimes spelled *kisha*), and *kisha* are used to give this sense of an expected event in a time frame. Forms of *kesh* always use the *ik-o* negation on the verb, never the *kiyo* form.

In modern usage, the *kesh* forms have somewhat fallen together in their usage. The forms are actually made from the conjunctions *cha* and *na*. In earlier speech, the *kisha* forms always marked the same subject in two clauses and *kina* forms marked different subjects. You will sometimes hear *kina* used, or simply *ki*.

The form *kesh* is used when no other conjunction appears with it:

    a.   Ak-peso kesh ia-li tuk.
         I hadn't seen him yet, so I left.
    b.   Hattakshali chik-apoksio kesh tʋmaha chik-io tuk.
         Since you haven't fixed the car yet, you haven't gone to town.
    c.   Akaka ak-awashlo kesh sa-hohchʋffoh alhi.
         Since I haven't fried the chicken yet, I'm really hungry.

Notice that the sense of the English *so* in example a. and of *since* in examples b. and c. are included in *kesh*.

Kesha or *kisha* is used when we want to add another conjunction, such as *kia* 'although', or when it appears at the end of the sentence:

    a.   Tʋmaha iachi kʋt ik-imanukfilo kesha.
         He hasn't thought about going to town yet.
    b.   Chik-toksalo kesha kia, iskʋlli ya ish-ishachi.
         Although you haven't worked yet, you'll get the money.
    c.   ". . . hattakshali ya ik-kashoffo kesha tok" (from chapter 3).
         Her car hadn't been cleaned even yet.

The following examples show *kisha* combined with the question markers o and a. Notice the different effects:

    a.   Ik-mihcho kisha.
         He hasn't done it yet.
    b.   Ik-mihcho kisha-ho? or Ik-mihcho kisho?
         Has he done it yet?
    c.   Ik-mihcho kisha?
         Hasn't he done it yet?

ANUMPA

Nouns

apolusli	[a-po-lús-li]	tire; casing
hina pʋtha	[hi-nʋ pʋt-hʋ]	paved road; highway
holisso itibapishi	[ho-lis-su i-ti-bá-pi-shi]	schoolmate
ivlli	[i-ʋl-li]	thing of value; money
lapalika	[lʋ-pa-li-ka]	the side
tʋli pʋtha	[tʋ-li pʋt-hʋ]	pavement

Verbs

abihli	[a-bih-li]	put on or insert plural things
im-alheka	[im-v-lhe-kv]	be painful to (Gp. 3)
itayokoma	[i-ta-yu-ko-mv]	scramble out; mixed up
maiya	[mai-yv]	go forward; pass
pvlhkichi	[pvlh-ki-chi]	cause to be fast; drive fast
polohlichi	[pu-loh-li-chi]	cause to spark
salahachi	[sv-la-hv-chi]	slow down
shanaioa	[shv-nai-o-wv]	weave; swerve
tvkohlit maya	[tv-koh-lit ma-yv]	be somewhere sporadically (pl)
yopomo	[yu-po-mu]	waste

Adverbs

mak fokali ma	[mak fo-ka-li ma]	at about that time

Idioms

ivlli isht ayopomo	waste money on
luak polohlochit pila	throw sparks
ome atokia	well; however; and so
pi hina ikpvtho	our lane

ANUMPA ANUKFILLI: Words for Loved Ones and Tree Names

Loved Ones

We all know how hard it is to find the right expression to indicate the exact relationship we have with those we care for. When is someone a *boyfriend* and not a *friend who is a boy*? In English there is a big distinction between romantic relationships and all others. In Choctaw, there is similar fuzziness in what might be meant by terms of endearment. The following are the most commonly used:

ikana is the most general term and can be used for any friend.
aiahni is a term denoting affection and esteem but does not imply romance.
i-hullo may be used for all loving relationships, including romantic ones.

ahinna is used for companionship and implies romance when used to refer to a couple.
ahalaia is a verb meaning 'to be concerned about in general'.
ahnichi means 'to like someone'.
aiokpạchi is a stronger term and implies a crush or infatuation.

There are a number of terms that one can use to mean 'a romantic partner'. The following terms refer to females, but *hattak* can be readily substituted:

ohoyo ahinna
ohoyo aiokpạchit ahinna
ohoyo ịhullot ahinna

Finally, we can use *ahinachi* to mean 'a caretaking companion in general'.

Tree Names

Here is a list of trees that grow natively in Choctaw homelands in both Mississippi and Oklahoma. Choctaw speakers you know may use other terms as well.

chisha	post oak
bʋyi	white oak from lowlands (*bʋyi* means 'swamp land')
chuahla	cedar
chishikta	red oak
oksak; uksak ʋpi	hickory
nosi ʋpi	oak (with acorns)
tiak	pine
sipsi	poplar
iti hika	gum tree
oksak hahe ʋpi	walnut
iti kʋfi	sassafras
chiskilik	black jack
oksak fʋla	pecan
sini	sycamore
ọkof	persimmon
chukcho	maple
tohto	elm

iti alikchi	cherry
iti ʋni	black gum
kʋti lʋkna	bois d'arc

Abʋchi

Chi-anukf<u>o</u>kah-<u>o</u>?

Translate the first paragraph of Mr. Tingle's story from Choctaw to English, using your own words. Notice how the choices were made with respect to vocabulary and phrasing. Do you like some of your own choices better?

Anumpa ʋlhpesa

A. Write four sentences in Choctaw that contain the sense of the English word *unless*. Use both *kiyo ahokma* and *ik-o . . . k m<u>a</u>* forms.

B. Write four more sentences in Choctaw that contain a negative comparison (the sense of the English *except*). Use both the *ketuk* form and the *illakato* forms, making sure you track the subject correctly.

C. Write another four Choctaw sentences that express the concept of *not . . . yet*.

D. What do these sentences mean?

1. Hattak shali himona iʋlli isht ayopomoh ik-sa-bʋnno.
2. Okla moma kʋt pʋlhkichi kia Sʋshki illakakosh ik-pʋlhkicho.
3. Ilhpak keyukm<u>a</u> nafohka ke-kancho ketuk.

Holissochi

Write a short piece in Chahta Anumpa, in any style, including at least two examples of the negative expressions *unless*, *except*, or *not yet*. Translate to Nahullo Anumpa.

CHAPTER 7

Ohoyo Lhamko 'A Strong Woman'

Choctaw Text and Translation: Ohoyo Lhamko 'A Strong Woman', by
Lois McAlvain Pugh

*Lois McAlvain Pugh of McAlester, Oklahoma, is the granddaughter of
Polk McAlvain, who was born in Mississippi, the son of Mary Mehahtubbee
and Scottish immigrant Benjamin McAlvain. Mary and her sons were
removed to Oklahoma in 1838 along the Trail of Tears as part of the great
displacement of southeastern Indians: Polk was sixteen years old. Mary
unfortunately died in a smallpox epidemic in Skullyville; her unmarked
grave has never been located. Polk McAlvain went on to become a well-to-do
stockman and landowner and was active politically in the Progressive Party,
which sponsored ownership of the land by individuals rather than by tribes
or other governmental entities. Polk's third wife was Louiza Bowers, Mrs.
Pugh's grandmother and a woman with a reputation for being elegant, high-
spirited, and unpredictable: she was also famous for her beautiful horses.
Here Mrs. Pugh tells about an exchange between husband and wife.*

Issuba humma palhki ichapa yosh, sapokni yʋt i̱-hiohlih beka tok—
svshki yʋt, itilaui ʋlhpesat itaichapa attok, achi tok. Issuba isht halʋlli
oklah shapulechik ma̱ aioklih fehna tok, micha iti chanaha aio̱binili tuklo
shali ya̱ ishthalʋllichi attok. Svshki yʋt, hʋshi hattakshali yʋt a̱sha fohka
ʋtta tokmʋt, palhki chʋfichi shahli ahinla tok, achi tok. Hina ya̱ peh
hopaki tobaklichi hosh isht a̱ya attok miya. Kʋna moma kʋt Lu Makalfin

66

ʋt mịti hokma, imatia oklah akuchachị kʋt ikhʋna tok. Yʋmmʋk attok kia, imissuba yạ kanima ishtiachị bʋnna tokmʋt, shapulahinla kạ ahni mʋt, yakni holitushi ʋlhtot ị-hioht mạya beka chatuk. Nittak hullo onnahinli achʋffa mạ ịhattak, Polk ʋt chukka ʋpishia binili tok, mihma ilapato tʋli pʋtha anowa nowat mịtih mʋt kanchak pit pisah ma issuba yʋt osapa kucha yạ mạya tok.

Sapokni ʋt nafohka achukma ạlhi hosh fohka chatok, achakanlichi kʋt chọkʋsh chaha fehna micha natikba hiket ishtia attok; ahokma Polk ato ịkana achukma yokmʋt nanishtʋtta apesachị kạ im-issa atok.

Atokọ achih mʋt, ibbak fohka faloha hochukma kash shuelit chukka yạ nowat ạyat chukka yạ onat, "Himmak tabokoli ontia kạ isht ia-lachị kạ ish-ikhana tok mihna kana't kucha weheli tuk." Yohmi kia kana hosh kucha weheli tokạ ikhana kiyu tok kanima, ʋlla kanimak atok kanima. Yohmi kia peh achi kʋt, "Ah, Lu yammak illa kạ! Nittak Hollo okma, peh imaiitanaha ia cha Chesus, ị-tahpala cha chukka ʋla cha nittak hollo mominchit alhip-ulli Polk Makalfin anumpa kʋllo onochit im-achị osh ohmi!

My grandmother had a fast team of bays—my mother said they were perfectly matched—they were beautiful in the harness, and she worked them to this two-seater carriage. Mama said that if she'd lived in the time of cars, she'd have been a speeder. She drove them just stretched-out down the road. Everybody knew to get out of her way when Lou McAlvain was coming. Well, anyway, she always kept them in the lot so she could harness them and take them when she wanted to. And coming in from church one Sunday morning, her husband Polk was sitting on the porch, and she was coming up the walk, and she looked at the barn, and the horses were out in the pasture.

My grandmother was always dressed extra nice, plus she was a very high-spirited and take-charge person, and Polk was easygoing, and he just let her. She managed most of the business.

And so she said, stripping off her long, elegant gloves as she walked to the house, "You knew I wanted to drive the horses this afternoon, and somebody's let them out." Well, I don't guess he knew who let them out, some of the boys, maybe. But he just said, "Oh, for that Lou! She just go to her church and shout to her Jesus on Sunday and come home and cuss at Polk McAlvain all week!"

Lois Pugh, with Choctaw translation by Henry Willis

Louiza Bowers McAlvain, wife of Polk McAlvain, and grandmother of Lois Pugh.
Date unknown. *Courtesy of Lois Pugh.*

Anumpa vlhpesa: Gradation, Comparison, and Equivalence

In this volume, as throughout the first volume of *Choctaw Language and Culture*, we have given the expressions that correspond to such English phrases as *too much* or *more than* as idioms each time they have appeared. This is because these notions are based on completely different concepts in Choctaw. We will examine those concepts in detail in this lesson.

'Too Much': *Atvpa* and *Atabli*

The sense of excessiveness or overdoing expressed by the English degree word *too* is expressed in Choctaw by the set of verbs *atvpa* and *atabli*. These verbs literally mean 'be beyond the cutoff point' (*atvpa*) or 'go beyond the cutoff point' (*atabli*). They are used in an important set of idiomatic expressions to convey the idea of excess.

atvpa and *atampa*

Atvpa and its stative form *atampa* are used to convey the sense of the English 'be too much'. They are used with the subordinator *kvt*. *Atvpa* is used to report new information or a change, while the stative *atampa* is used to state what is known or constant. Remember that these aspects simply give a point of view about the way something is perceived in time (see chapter 15 in *Choctaw Language and Culture*).

    a. Chi-chunna kvt atampa.
       You are too skinny.
    b. vlla mvt liteha kvt atvpa.
       That child is too dirty.
    c. Lvshpa kvt atampa.
       It's too hot.
    d. Tvmaha ish-iachih-o?
       —Kiyo, sa-tikahbi kvt atvpa.
       Are you going to town?
       —No, I'm too tired.

It is important to note that *atvpa* and *atampa* never take person markers themselves—they always appear "bare." The person marker, if there is one, instead appears in the first clause, on the word that names the quality that is excessive. Very often this will be an adjective or a Group 2 verb, that is, one that has an affected subject (see chapter 7 in

Choctaw Language and Culture). Notice, for instance, that example d. literally means "I'm tired, past the cut-off point."

atabli

Atabli is a Group 1 verb (one that has an agent subject) that is used when the idea of 'doing to excess' is expressed. Again, the subordinator *kvt* is used to join the part of the sentence that expresses what is over-done. The verb *atabli* is different from *atvpa* because it takes person markers. *Atabli* may often appear in its stative form, *atambli,* when one refers to an ongoing state of affairs.

    a. Taloa kvt atabli-li.
       I sing too much. (*Or* I overdo my singing.)
    b. Hattak mvt impa kvt atambli.
       That man is eating too much. (stative aspect)
    c. Aki vt toksali kvt atabli.
       My father works too much.
    d. Anufilli kvt ish-atabli.
       You think too much.

A variant of *atabli* is *atablichi,* which simply adds the causative marker *-chi* and is similar in meaning:

Nusi kvt il-atablichi.
We sleep too much.

Note the difference between the following two sentences:

    a. Anumpa ikbi falayachi kvt atabli.
       He's making the speech too long. (*Or* He's overdoing it making the speech long.)
    b. Anumpa ikbi yvt falaya kvt atampa.
       The speech is too long.

Idioms of the Type "Too . . . to . . ." (e.g., "Too Tired to Play")

Sometimes we want to include an activity relevant to *being too much*: being too tired to swim, too excited to sleep, and so on. In Choctaw we make another clause marked with *kʋt* that names the activity that has been deemed impossible, and continue as before:

> ʋlla mʋt washohachi̱ kʋt tikahbi kʋt atapa.
> That child is too tired to play. (Literally, "The child would play, he's tired past the cut-off point."

Notice the order of the clauses and the form of the verb in the example above. The future marker -*achi̱* appears on the verb *washoha* because the child did not actually play, the playing was hypothetical. The clause containing *washoha* appears first, followed by the clause naming the quality that was excessive, and last is a form of *atʋpa*.

It is preferable to place person markers on the verb in the first clause (the one that names the activity) as well as on the adjective in the second clause (the one that names the quality that is excessive):

> a. Ish-toksalachi̱ kʋt chi̱-takobi kʋt atampa.
>   You're too lazy to work.
> b. Hika-lachi̱ kʋt sa-nia kʋt atampa.
>   I'm too fat to fly.
> c. Issoba mʋt pi-pi̱sachi̱ kʋt sipokni kʋt atampa.
>   That horse is too old to see us.

When we *do* something to excess, we use *atabli* or *atablichi*:

> d. Hash-balilachi̱ kʋt impa kʋt hash-atabli tuk.
>   You ate too much to run.

Comparison: *I̱-shahli* and *I̱-shahlichi*

When two states or actions are being directly compared, English has an idiomatic construction that goes along the lines of *more . . . than . . . .* For example, we can say that my dog is bigger than yours, or I fry chicken better than you do, or your house is more beautiful than his house. In Choctaw, we do something completely different: we have special verbs that appear in their own clauses, with the comparison in another clause joined by *kʋt*, just as we did with *atʋpa*. These verbs are *i̱-shahli* and *i̱-shahlichi*. Literally, they mean 'to surpass' or 'to be superior to' (*i̱-shahli*) and 'to do surpassingly' or 'to outdo' (*i̱-shahlichi*).

I̲-shahli

This verb is used to make comparisons between states of being and qualities, typically adjectives. The person or thing that is being compared as lesser is marked with the recipient person marker. The person or thing that is being compared as greater is marked with the agent person marker.

Chaha kvt is-sa̲-shahli.
You are taller than me. (*Or* You are taller than I am.)

In the example above, we first name the quality being compared, *chaha* 'tall', and set it off with *kvt*. Then we mark the person who is taller, *ish-* (appearing here in the form *is-*), as the subject, and the person who is less tall with the recipient marker *sa̲*. Literally, this sentence might be: "As for being tall, you surpass me."

   a. Nuktala kvt chi̲-shahli-li.
      I am wiser than you.
   b. Ohoyo mvt nukoa kvt pi̲-shahli.
      That woman is angrier than us. (*Or* That woman is angrier than we are.)
   c. A̲hattak vt chunna kvt i̲ki i̲-shahli.
      My husband is skinnier than his father.
   d. Issoba pvt ayukli kvt inla ma̲ i̲-shahli.
      This horse is handsomer than that other one.

I̲-shahlichi

When we compare actions, "doing" rather than "being," we use the verb *i̲-shahlichi*, which is used precisely the same way as *i̲-shahli*. The meaning of *i̲-shahlichi* is very much like the English 'to outdo':

Taloa kvt is-sa̲-shahlichi tuk.
You outsang me. (*Or* You outdid me in singing.)

But often we wish to name another quality as a basis of comparison, such as *better, more, longer,* and the like. Then we need to use a verb telling what that basis is. The commonest verbs to use are *achukmali* for 'better' or *lawachi* for 'do more':

   a. Taloah achukmali kvt is-sa̲-shahlichi.
      You sing better than I do. (*Or* In singing well, you outdo me.)

b. Taloah lawachi kʋt chi̱-shahlichi-li.
   I sing more than you do. (*Or* In singing a lot, I outdo you.)
c. Pipokni ʋt taloah chitoli kʋt hapi̱-shahlichi.
   Our grandma sings louder than we do. (*Or* In singing loudly, Grandma outdoes us all.)

More things

When we want to talk about comparing things rather than actions or states of being, we must make a rather complicated construction using *lawa* and a form of *i̱-shahli* or *i̱-shahlichi*. We need a clause for the thing being compared, one for the quality being compared, and another for the act of "being superior."

Here are two ways to say "You bought more peaches than I did":

a. Takkon chompa-li ka̱, lawa kʋt a̱-shahli-ho̱ ish-chompa-tuk.
   This sentence could be literally translated something like "You bought, exceeding me in the number of peaches I bought".
b. Takkon lʋwah chompa-li ka̱ is-sa̱-shahlichi hosh ish-chompa tuk.
   This sentence could be literally translated something like, "You bought, outdoing me in buying a lot of peaches."

Superlatives Using *I̱-shahli*

We may use *i̱-shahli* and especially its intensive form *i̱-shaiali* when we wish to express something to an extreme degree. These forms may often be best translated with the English superlative (*-est* or *most*). Notice that in these cases, the comparison is understood but unmentioned, so there is no need for a separate clause naming the quality of comparison. These forms may be written without a hyphen.

a. ". . . imʋlhpichik chaha i̱shahli . . ." (from chapter 24, *Choctaw Language and Culture*).
   the highest nest
b. Hattak nuktala i̱shaiali ya̱ il-itanaha tuk.
   We met the wisest man.

Comparison of Adjectives Using the *-h-* Form

In Choctaw, besides the constructions with *i̱-shahli*, we have another way of comparing two things with respect to some quality. This way makes use of the same form as the one used to form the momentaneous aspect in verbs. You may recall that the forms that mark the stative aspect and the resolutional aspect in verbs also mark the intensive form in adjectives; so does the *-h-* infix of the momentaneous aspect form the comparative in adjectives.

 a. Nita chihto mvt nvni moma ka̱ ilaieshi.
    That bigger bear took all the fish for himself.
 b. Issoba luhsa ma̱ aiokpa̱chi-li.
    I like that blacker horse.

When we use this form, we are commenting on one of two things with a quality that is being used to distinguish them.
     Compare the following forms of *chito*:

chito	big
chihto	bigger
chi̱to	very big
chieto	excessively big

     However, if we compare things directly, in sentences that require *than* in English, we must use *i̱-shahli*:

Nita mvt chito kvt inla i̱-shahli.
That bear is bigger than the other one.

Equivalence

     The last relationship we will study in this lesson is the equivalency relation expressed in English by *as . . . as.* The student may have guessed that this relation will be handled by a related set of verbs as well. These verbs are *lauechi*, which means roughly 'to equal'; *itilauichi* 'to match; to be equal to each other'; and *alauichi* 'to be equal in number'. (The slight variation in spelling is due to the fact that in *lauechi*, the second syllable is stressed, causing the vowel to be lengthened, with *i* becoming *e*.)

Lauechi and *itilauichi*
Lauechi is used to express equivalent qualities or actions:

 a. Nita hochvffo ya̱ hochvffo-kvt lauechi-li.
    I am as hungry as a bear.

b. Taloah chi̱-punna kʋt is-sa-lauechi.
   You sing as well as I do.
c. Hattak mʋt taloah i̱-punna kʋt chi-lauechi.
   That man sings as well as you do.

In example a., we first describe the hungry bear, then say, in effect, "as for being hungry, I equal it."

Often we use the reciprocal marker *iti* to indicate that one is equal to the other:

a. Nanikhʋna kʋt chitilauichi-li. *(chi + itilauichi)*
   You are as intelligent as I am. (*Or*, "I am as intelligent as you are."
   This sentence might be literally translated as "As for being intelligent, you and I are equal to each other".)
b. Hattak ilʋppʋt toksali kʋt hattak achʋffa ma̱ itilauichi.
   This man works as much as that other one.

Alauichi

Sometimes we need to talk about the equivalence of things rather than states or actions. The variant form *alauichi* is used in these cases.

a. Palʋska lʋwa ish'pa kʋt is-s'alauichi.
   You ate as much bread as I did.
b. Ohoyo yʋmmʋt aboha lʋwa kashoffi kʋt achʋffa ma̱ alauichi tuk.
   That woman cleaned as many rooms as the other one did.

Laue, itilaui, and *alaui*

A set of adjectives—*laue* (*lauwi*) 'equal', *itilaui* 'matched', and *alaui* 'equal; adequate'—have the same central meanings as the verbs and are used to modify nouns in noun phrases.

". . . sʋshki yʋt, itilaui ʋlhpesat itaichapa attok, achi tok."
Mother said they were a perfectly matched team.

ANUMPA

Nouns

atia	[á-ti-yʋ]	way; passage
chukka ʋpishia	[chuk-kʋ ʋ-pi-shé-ʋ]	porch

chvfichi	[chv-fí-chi]	driver
ibbak fohka	[ib-bak fóh-kv]	gloves
ichapa	[i-chá-pv]	team
nanishtvtta	[na-nisht-vt-tv]	business
nittak hollo	[nit-tak hól-lu]	week
tvli pvtha anowa	[tv-li pvt-hv a-nó-wv]	paved walkway
tabokoli ontia	[tv-bó-ku-li ot-iv]	afternoon
yakni holitushi	[yak-ni ho-li-tú-shi]	lot; pen

Verbs

vlhto	[vlh-tu]	stand in; be in (plural)
alauichi	[v-lau-i-chi]	do equally
im-issa	[im-is-sv]	to let; permit; offer (recipient object)
itilauichi	[i-ti-lau-i-chi]	do the same as each other
i-hiohli	[i-hi-oh-li]	have plural things (Gp. 3)
onochi	[o-nu-chi]	send on; inflict
shapulechi	[sha-pu-le-chi]	work in a harness
tabaklichi	[tv-bák-li-chi]	gallop
weheli, weli	[we-he-li]	take out plural things

Adjectives

alaui	[a-lau-i]	equal; adequate
itaichapa, itachapa	[i-ta-i-cha-pv]	paired up together
itilaui	[i-te-lau-i]	matched
faloha	[fv-ló-hv]	long (plural)
hochukma	[ho-chúk-mv]	good (plural)
laue, lauwi	[lau-e]	equal
shapoli, shapuli	[sha-po-li]	laden; burdened; harnessed

Adverbs

| itilaui vlhpesa | [i-te-lau-i vlh-pe-sv] | perfectly |
| shahli | [shah-li] | excessively |

Conjunction

    mihna   [mih-na]   and then; and so; therefore

Idioms

akachanlichi	[a-kv-chá-li-chi]	plus; in addition
chokvsh chaha	high-spirited	
ikana achukma	easygoing	
kvna moma	everybody	
natikba hiket ishtia	the one who takes charge	
pvlhki chvfichi shahli	speeder (excessively fast driver)	
tikba hiket ishtia	take charge	

Anumpa Anukfilli: Plural Words

Recall that Choctaw does not have a formal grammatical marker, such as s, for plural nouns, but it has a multitude of other ways to indicate that a thing is plural. One very common way is to include plural subjects or objects in the meanings of verbs. Here are a few examples of some of those verbs:

Plural Subject

vlhto	stand in or be in
takohlit maya	be somewhere sporadically
bachoha	be in rows or courses
heli	fly

Plural Object

bohli	lay things down
i-hiohli	have things
weheli, weli	take out things
abihli	put in things
lhilahli	be torn in pieces

Plural Adjectives

Another kind of plural word in Choctaw is the adjective that refers only to plural nouns. Some of these are:

faloha	long	(compare: falaya, singular)
hochukma	good	(compare: achukma)
chipinta	small	(compare: ossi)
hochito	big	(compare: chito)

Others

There are other words that are compounded with a noun and a verb or adjective where the plural form of the compound is marked in the modifying verb or adjective. One interesting case is the Choctaw for 'island.' This compound literally means "land that appears as a patch in a background." The verb that means 'one thing is a patch in a background' is *tashayi*, but the verb that means 'several things appear as patches in a background' is *talhkachi*.

yakni tashaya	island
yakni talhkachi	islands
peni hika	airplane
peni heli	airplanes

Abvchi

Chi-anukfokah-o?

Examine the storytelling style that Mrs. Pugh uses, and the Choctaw that Mr. Willis uses to translate it. What do the Choctaw words literally mean? Discuss the problems of translating an artistic form from one language to another.

Anumpa vlhpesa

A. Write ten sentences expressing the concept of *too* or *too much*. Be sure to use forms of both *atvpa* and *atabli*.

B. Write ten sentences expressing the concept of comparison. Pay attention to the difference in *i̱-shahli* and *i̱-shahlichi*. Make a comparison using the *-h* insertion in adjectives.

C. Write ten sentences expressing the concept of equivalence. Use *lauechi, itilauichi,* and *alauichi* and understand their different uses.

D. What do these sentences mean?

1. Peni heli yʋt hochito kʋt hattak shali i̱-shahli.
2. Ibbak fohka ilʋppʋt faloha kʋt atampa.
3. Issuba tuklo yʋt balili pʋlhki hosh itilauichi.

E. Write five sentences using a verb or adjective that is always plural in its meaning. Translate to Nahullo Anumpa.

Holissochi

Write a story in Chahta Anumpa about a family member that has been told to you. Translate to Nahullo Anumpa.

CHAPTER 8

Nefa, Nahoyo Impunna
'Neva, the Hunter'

Choctaw Text and Translation: *Nefa, Nahoyo Impunna* 'Neva, the Hunter', by Lois McAlvain Pugh

Neva McAlvain Bryan was a cousin to both Lois McAlvain Pugh and Jay McAlvain; they shared their grandfather Polk McAlvain, the husband of Louiza Bowers, the strong woman from chapter 7. Besides her famous relationship with automobiles, Aunt Neva was known as a crack marksman and hunter. Here Lois McAlvain Pugh tells of a particular squirrel that met up with Aunt Neva one fateful day.

Nefa yvt vlla nakni vlheha issi ibahoyot ia atok. Oklah issi vbi keyu mako ilap ato vbi beka tok. Hossa kvt impunna attok. Fvni vbi imma ka peh hachim-anoli-li yo pulla makachi.

Okla haknip achukma imma itoksali moma kvt, tanap nihi pokoli tuklo akucha tuklo nashali anoka shalit isht aya chatuk. Naki lumbo hokli tanapo akuchi cha akka patvlhpo bohlih atok. Atoko himmona ma vlla naknossi, afvmmi auah tuklo, itolat shakba kobaffi toko, tvmaha Nusvpi Humma ont ahoyo cha Tvlihina, shakba hakmo apolusli toka pisachi ho isht ia tok. Ayant okla ma, fvni yvt hina tikba vbanampoli pisa cha nashali ash yokopachih mvt, "Saso, himmak, yohmi ahni fehna hosh—pvlhkit kanali keyu hosh—tanamp naki lumbo aialhto ma et ama." Mihma et ima tok, mihma shvlali-chit tanampo pit fohkih, okhisushi apisa akka litohkachit tiwih mvt, tanampo ma owelih mvt fvni ya apisalit hossat iti ya pit aiakachi tok.

80

"Peh, a-himonat aki ont ak-im-anoli na. Ohoyo sipokni chishno ohmi hosh apisalit hossat fvni vbit kanchi tok, ont im-achi-lachi̱!" vllanakni vt achi tok.

Fvni yash o̱ Tvlihina ishtona tok, abeka aiasha ma alikchi yvmma vtta kvt fvni achvffa ayukali vbi ka bvnna atok. Hoponik mvt—i-champuli attok. Kanima nana ikabunno aiashachi atokma, fvni ma isht ia cha fvni yvmma alhofih mvt ahoponi ishiat mvlha ont hoyo cha fvni ma fokki cha achefat ishih mvt, "Ilap ato Alikchi Yvmmak i̱ micha Yvmak im-iahoke."

Neva would go deer hunting with her boys. They wouldn't get a deer, but she would. She was a good marksman—I have to tell you about her killing squirrels.

When she was a community health worker, she always carried her .22 rifle in the car with her. She'd take the magazine out and put it down there on the floor. And so once she had to go get this little boy, twelve years old, down by Red Oak and take him to Talihina, to have a cast checked on his arm: he had fallen and broken an arm. And so she saw this squirrel running across the road, so she stops the car, and she says, "Sonny, reach down there very carefully now—don't move fast—and get the magazine for my gun. And he handed it to her, and she slipped it into the gun, rolled the window glass down, and pointed that gun, and shot that squirrel right out of that tree.

And the boy said, "Just wait 'til I tell my dad. An old woman like you just dead-eyed that squirrel!"

And she took the squirrel over to Talihina—there was a doctor over there at the hospital who wanted every one she could get: he cooked them; he liked them. And so, she went out to where the dump was, and skinned that squirrel, and went to the kitchen and got a pan, put it in there, washed it, took it and said, "This goes to Doctor So-and-So."

Lois McAlvain Pugh, with Choctaw by Henry Willis

ANUMPA VLHPESA: Moods and Possessive Predicates

Mood

In language, there are many ways to indicate the speaker's attitude as well as the content of the speech itself. This is called the *mood*, and we have looked at some moods in Choctaw already. There is the mood used when reporting (called the *indicative* by grammarians), the mood used when something is not real or hasn't happened yet (we mark this with *-k* and a future tense marker), the potential mood, for talking about things that might happen, and the imperative mood, in which the speaker commands.

Let

Besides the command forms that are used to directly tell someone else what to do or not do, there are more general forms that may also concern the speaker and persons not present. In English, we use the verb *let* to perform this function. Grammarians use the terms *imperative* or *hortative* to describe this mood. (*Hortative* has the same root as *exhort*, to urge someone to do something.)

Let's eat.
Let's not go to Marlo's party.
Let me watch this program.
Let them do it themselves.
Let him try to do it.

In Choctaw, this mood is marked with the set of *ik-* person markers used in negation. But rather than changing the final vowel of the verb stem to *-o*, we leave the verb stem as is. Instead, we place an accent on that vowel, just as we do in commands. Just to illustrate, a written accent has been placed in the following examples. Notice that we don't use this mood with the second person, *you*. Those would be straightforward commands.

a. Ak-chukkoá.
   Let me come in!
b. Ik-chukkoá.
   Let him/her/it come in!
c. Ke-chukkoá.
   Let's come in!
d. Oklah ik-chukkoá.
   Let them come in!

We attach other person markers (affected and recipient) in their usual position before the verb stem and after the *ik* subject marker. To put verbs together with other verbs or other kinds of predicates, we use the -*t* form, as we have seen again and again. (In written Choctaw, the final accent is usually omitted. It does appear in the New Testament.)

"... aki ont ak-im-anoli ..."
Let me go and tell my father ...

Group 2 and 3 verbs
These verbs take the same subject markers as their negative counterparts, *ik* with the affected or recipient subject marker. The final vowel of the verb stem is accented.

a. Ik-illi.
   Let him die.
b. Ik-si-anukfohka.
   Let me understand.
c. Ik-pim-anukfila.
   Let us be mindful.

Summary of Choctaw Moods

Indicative
The indicative mood describes things that are factual, but it also includes questions. On verbs, we frequently see the predicative *h* as a connector. Many writers include the *h* as a present tense marker as well.

a. Mvlha himona chompa-li tuk.
   I bought a new pan.
b. Katimma ish-ia?
   Where are you going?
c. Nita hossah mvt iki i-tahpala tuk.
   After he shot the bear, he called to his father.

Hypothetical and other moods of indistinct time
When we need to talk about things that haven't happened yet, hadn't yet happened in the past ("future in the past"), or might have happened at some indistinct time in the past, we must use different tense and mood markers. In Choctaw, verbs and other predicates are very often marked

with <u>k</u>, which is frequently translated as 'if'. We most often use the *-achi̲*
future marker to indicate that something hasn't actually happened. (The
terms *subjunctive* and *irrealis* are often used to talk about these moods in
other languages.)

- a. Fvni pa̲ alho̲ffachi̲. (marked with *-achi̲*)
  He will skin this squirrel.
- b. Fvni ya̲ alho̲ffi-lachi̲tuk kia abekat sa-toba tuk. (future in the past:
  -achi̲tuk)
  I was going to skin the squirrel, but I got sick.
- c. Naknossi vt hofantik mvt alikchi tobah bvnna. ('when' in the future:
  -k mvt)
  When the little boy grows up, he wants to become a doctor.
- d. "Atoko̲ himmona ma̲ vlla naknossi . . . shakba hakmo apolusli toka̲
  pisachi̲ ho̲ isht ia tok."
  And so once she took a little boy to get the cast on his arm checked.

In example d., the future tense marker is on the verb *pisa* ('look at' or
'check') to indicate that the cast had not yet been looked at, it was going
to be looked at (future in the past).

Potential, or '*be able to*'
A very important mood in Choctaw is the one that indicates things
that could happen, might happen, or should happen. This mood has a
number of markers that are attached to the verb stem. Choctaw also has
negative mood markers, placed in the same position.

The following are potential mood markers that appear attached to
the verb stem:

ahinla	can
ahinla tuk; tok	could; could have
ahekeyu	could not; will not
ahe	ought; should
ahinlachi̲	will be able to
ahinlahe	was supposed to have

- a. Ilhpak moma ka̲ weheli-lahinla.
  I can take out all the groceries.
- b. Is-si-apelahinla tuk.
  You could have helped me.

c. "... imissuba ya kanima ishtiachi̱ bvnna tokmvt, shapulahinla ka̱
   ahni.... chatuk" (from chapter 7).
   She could (would be able to) take her horses out when she wanted
   and harness them ...
d. Aiatokko il-onahekeyu tuk.
   We couldn't reach the shelter.
e. Naknossi vt himmita kvt atampa cha naki lumbo chompahekeyu.
   The little boy is too young and so he can't buy bullets.

We may also use *kanima* at the end of the clause, together with another
mood marker such as *achi* or *ahinla* to give the sense of 'may' or 'might'. We
can use *kanima* by itself to mean 'perhaps' or 'maybe'.

a. Svshki vt shulosh himona chompa ka̱ am-issachi̱ kanima.
   Mom might let me buy new shoes.
b. "Yohmi kia kana hosh kucha weheli toka̱ ikhana kiyo tuk kanima,
   vlla kanimak attok kanima." (from chapter 7)
   Well, he perhaps didn't know who let them out, it was some boy
   maybe.

Emphatic mood markers

Choctaw also uses markers to indicate emphasis: we have learned *oke*
'is indeed', and *-shke* 'does indeed'. We also have a negative form of *-shke*,
kashke, which is not easily translated but means something like 'does not'.
(There is more about *kashke* in chapter 9.) These emphatic markers
appear last, after the tense marker, putting them at the end of the clause
or sentence.

a. Lvshpa tokoke!
   It was indeed hot!
b. "Iloh i̱-yimmashke" (vba isht taloa #4, *Choctaw Hymn Book*).
   We do indeed believe in him.

In Choctaw we may use mood markers along with aspectual adverbs
such as *pulla* 'have to, must' and aspect-marked verbs to make very finely
articulated statements:

Ish-hoho̱yoh pullashke!
You do have to keep looking for it!

In the example above, there is iterative aspect on *hoyo*, the aspectual adverb *pulla*, and emphatic *shke*.

Ish-hoho̲yoh poyyollashke!
You do absolutely have to keep looking for it!

In the above example, there is additionally intensive marking on *pulla* to produce *poyyolla* 'absolutely have to'.

We may also negate *shke* with *kiyo/keyu:*

Il-ikhanah kiyoshke.
We *do not* know.

If we use *kashke*, we need to use the *ik-o* negative form:

Kil-ikhano kashke.
We *do not* know.

Possessive predicates

We have learned to attach possessive markers to nouns to show possession, as in *amofi, chi̲holisso*, and *pishki*. We may also show possession in the predicate with special forms of pronouns, corresponding to the English forms *mine, yours, his, hers, its,* and *theirs*.

ammi, ѵmmi	mine
chimmi	yours
immi	his; hers; its; theirs
pimmi	ours
hapimmi	all of ours
hachimmi, hѵchimmi	yours (plural)
itimmi	each other's

a. Holisso ilѵppѵt ammi.
   This book is mine.
b. Ofi hohchѵfo ѵt chimmi.
   That hungry dog is yours.
c. Hattak tuklo mѵt nanishtshila itimmi i̲shi.
   The two men have got each other's towels.

ANUMPA

Nouns

aiatokko	[ai-*v*-tók-ku]	shelter
m*v*lha	[m*v*-lh*v*]	tin pan
naki lumbo	[na-ki lúm-bu]	bullet
naknossi	[nak-nós-si]	little boy
nana ikab*v*nno aiashachi	[na-n*v* ik-*v*-b*v*n-no ai-á-sh*v*-chi]	dump
tilikpi; tilihpi	[ti-lík-pi]	shield

Verbs

*v*banapoli	[*v*-b*v*-na-pu-li]	jump over; pass over
alh<u>o</u>ffi, alh<u>u</u>ffi	[a-lh<u>o</u>f-fi]	skin; strip hide from
kanali	[ka-na-li]	move
lhitohkachi	[lhi-toh-k*v*-chi]	rewind; loosen by winding; roll down
<u>o</u>weli	[<u>o</u>-we-li]	aim a gun at

Idioms

okla haknip achukma imma <u>i</u>toksali	community health worker
iti y<u>a</u> pit aiakachi	right out of that tree
tanap nihi pokoli tuklo akucha tuklo	.22 caliber rifle
naki lumbo hokli	magazine of gun
saso	term of address: boy; kid
Y*v*mmak <u>i</u> micha Y*v*mmak	So-and-So

ANUMPA ANUKFILLI: *Inli*

This important and very abstract marker indicates the moment or the present, and can be compared to the *ash* particle, which marks the past or that which has already been mentioned. *Inli* may be put directly onto words, especially time words, or it may be compounded, particularly to make *akinli* and *makinli*. Like many other words in Choctaw, *inli* changes its meaning depending on the class of the word which it modifies.

a. Himmakinli ia-lachi̠.
    I'll be going just now.
b. Onnahinli omba.
    It's raining this morning.

Inli may be put with pronouns to form the emphatic '*oneself*':

Ilap inli akosh wak moma ka̠ ipeta.
He himself is feeding all the cattle.

When compounded with *mak* this word appears with nouns to mean '*the same*':

a. Hushi makinli ho̠ yokachi tuk.
    He caught the same bird.
b. Nittak makinli ho̠ ia tuk.
    He went on the same day.

When compounded with *ak*, this word has two different uses in the predicate, depending on whether it is used with adjectives or with verbs. *Akinli* is one of the few adverbials that appears *after* the predicate. With predicate adjectives, *akinli* means 'also', 'too', or 'as well'.

a. ꙳no ato achukmah akinli.
    I am fine also.
b. ꙳llatek m꙳t pisachukmah akinli.
    That girl is pretty too.
c. Iti ꙳t apissah akinli.
    The stick is also straight.

When used after verbs, *akinli* is best translated as 'again', or, since it most often appears with the future marker, as simply the future tense:

a. Apela-lachi̠ akinli.
    I'll help him (in the future).
b. Himmak apela-lachi̠ akinli.
    I'll help him now.
c. Onnakma pi̠sa-lachi̠ akinli.
    I'll be seeing him again tomorrow.

Abⱱchi

Chi-anukfo̱kah-o̱?

Return to the Choctaw conversations in the story. Try to translate them in your own words. Pay attention to the particles that indicate the tone of the conversation.

Anumpa ⱱlhpesa

A. Make a sentence and write it in the Choctaw indicative mood, the "not real" or subjunctive mood, the potential mood, and the emphatic mood. Each mood has several varieties; you may choose among them. How does the sentence change each time? Translate to Nahullo Anumpa.

B. Translate these possessive predicates to Chahta Anumpa.

1. This rifle is mine.
2. The cucumbers on that table are yours.
3. Is this tin pan hers?
4. That tent might be ours.
5. That money is indeed yours.
6. The little boys played with each other's puppies.

C. What do these sentences mean?

1. Hattak shali ilⱱppⱱt salaha kⱱt atampa hosh hattak shali inla maiyahekeyu kashke.
2. Naknossi akosh iti naksish ⱱbanapolachi̱ akinli.

Holissochi

Write a short story in Chahta Anumpa that uses the potential mood, the emphatic mood, and the "not real" mood at least once each. Translate to Nahullo Anumpa.

CHAPTER 9

Ahollopi 'The Gravehouse'

Choctaw Text and Translation: *Ahollopi* 'The Gravehouse', by Grayson Noley

Grayson Noley, a professor and a fine storyteller, has shared a number of his father's stories, many of them humorous, as in this one about getting caught in a storm in just the wrong place. This is the story as it was told to and recorded by Tim Tingle, the Choctaw folklorist.

Kaniohmi ho, Chahta yʋt ahollopi ia chatuka ish-ikhanah- o? . . . Ikana ya inowat aya tok, miya. ʋba yʋmma hoshonti chito pit pisa tok, miya. Ichuka yʋt tikba hopaki ho nanombinilit onachi tokosh, "Yohmi atoko ia-li makila. Hoshonti mʋt bilika ʋlah aialhi fehna. Achuka onah sa-bʋnna. Si-on-omba yo sa-bʋnna keyu," achi tok. Atokosh imissuba tolloblit ombinilih mʋt ichuka balilichi hosh ia tok. Yohmi kia hoshonti yʋmmʋt, palhki kʋt cheki na mitit apaknakachi tok. Ombinilit palhkichit isht ia tomba ma ombat isht ia tok. Ahollopi ont ia hosh aya fokali ma omba chitoli aialhi tok. Atoko, "Yʋmma, ikhana-li, peh isht ona-lish micha ahollopi chukushi tolublit nuta pit chukoa-lachi," achi tok.

Atoko ombinilit ayah momat tolloblit issuba akkowa cha toshpa hosh kapali isht talakchi iti nakshish afohommi cha yʋmma iat onah mʋt ahollopi chukushi ʋba wakelit tushpa hosh nuta tolublit pit chukoa tok, ont chukoa ma anuka ilappʋt ashila achukma tok; chukushi ilappʋt ashilak mʋt achukma tok. Atoko yʋmma binili na alhchihba tuk, achi tok. Chekusih ma

90

issuba inla yosh balilih palʋmmichi hosh ʋla ka̱ ha̱klo tuk. Palhki hosh ant yokopali tok. Issuba ombinili achʋffakash osh yʋmma filemoat pit pisah mʋt yʋmmak kia kapali isht talakchi pit ʋbanʋblichit pilla tok. Balilit iat ahollopi chukushi makashinli ho̱ ʋba wakeli tok. ʋba wakelih mʋt balalit chukoat ishtiah fehna mah; mihma a̱ki yʋt, "Satibapishi ma, peh ant chukoa. Ilappa̱ ashila fehnahoke!" achi tok miya.

You know how Choctaws used to go to these gravehouses? He (my father) said he was visiting his friend. He said he looked up and a big thunderhead was there. He said he had a long way to ride before he'd get home, so he said, "Well, I better take off. That thunderhead's getting pretty close. I want to get home. I don't want to get rained on." So he jumped on his horse and took off, went riding home. But that cloud moved fast and it was over him pretty soon. He started riding fast and it started raining. It was raining hard, just as he was going by a cemetery. So he said, "Yeah, I know, I'll just ride up and jump under this gravehouse."

So he was riding along and he jumped off his horse, and quick threw the reins around a limb and went over there and pulled up the gravehouse. He went in there and it was nice and dry, nice and dry in this gravehouse. So, he said he was sitting there for a little while. And pretty soon, he heard this other horse come running hard. He said it pulled up real fast and stopped. The rider looked there and threw his reins over, too. He started running over and picked the same gravehouse. He picked it up and started crawling in. And my father said, "Come on in, brother; it sure is dry in here!"

Grayson Noley, with Choctaw translation by Henry Willis

ANUMPA ʋLHPESA: More on Negation: *Never*, *Any*, and Other Negative Expressions

We already know that Choctaw has several ways of negating words, phrases, and clauses, all of them different from what we do in English. Here we will learn how to make negations that correspond to such ideas as *any*, *none*, and *never*.

Negating Nouns: *Not . . . any*

One way that English negates noun phrases is by using the negator *not* followed by the word *any*, which modifies the noun:

I don't see anyone.
I didn't make anything.
You didn't eat any dinner.

Choctaw uses a system that always employs a negated verb. When we want to talk about indefinite negatives, such as *anyone* or *anywhere*, we use the indefinites plus *kia* along with a negated verb. It is more common to use a form of the *ik-o* negative, but we may also use *kiyo*.

a. Kanah kia ak-peso.
   I don't see anyone. (Literally, "I didn't see someone." Choctaw does not make a distinction between *anyone* and *someone* the way English does.)
b. Kanimmah kia kil-io tuk.
   We didn't go anywhere.
c. Nana kia chik-ikbo.
   You didn't make anything.
d. Issi kanohmih kia hachik-hosso.
   You (pl.) didn't shoot many deer.
e. ". . . kana yʋt cheki na ʋlat apelachi kiyo . . ." (from chapter 22, *Choctaw Language and Culture*)
   . . . when no one would come to help . . . (Literally, "when someone wouldn't come to help")
f. Takkon chito ak-chompo.
   I didn't buy any apples.

In example f. we need not mark *takkon chito* in any particular way. The negated verb is all that is needed.

We are much likelier to use one of the many definiteness markers (refer to chapter 11) to mark a negated noun phrase, depending on whether it is new or old information, part of a specified group, and other factors:

Takkon chito ka ak-chompo.
I didn't buy any of the apples.

Kana keyu: No one

We may also use *kana keyu* to mean 'no one', especially if the expression is freestanding, that is, not in a sentence. *Kana keyu* is not normally used in sentences.

"Kata hosh chi-pisat ayachi?" "Kana keyu."
"Who is going to visit you?" "No one."

Not having

Recall that in Choctaw there are special verbs that are used when we talk about not having, or there being a lack of something. The most used are *iksho* 'there isn't any' (Gp. 2) and *ikimiksho* 'one doesn't have (any)' (Gp. 3).

    a. Paki okchi hosh iksho.
       There isn't any grape juice.
    b. Iskvlli ik-sam-iksho.
       I don't have any money.

Ever and Never

In Choctaw we have a somewhat more complicated way of expressing the ideas of something that does not happen habitually over time, and something that has not happened even once over a period of time. We will introduce two mood markers to do this. Note that in English the word *never* and a tense marker are all that is necessary to accomplish this.

Chatok kiyo 'Never in the past'

    a. Hattak mvt chi-apela chatok-o?
       Did that man ever help you?
    b. Hattak mvt si-apela chatok kiyo.
       That man never helped me.

In example b., *chatok* 'ever' is negated with *kiyo*. The meaning is that there was not a time in the past when that man helped me.

chatoshba 'never habitually'

    a. Ohoyo mvt chi-apela chatosh-o?
       Does that woman ever help you?
    b. Ohoyo mvt si-apela chatoshba.
       That woman never helps me.

In the second example, the idea is that the woman makes a habit of not helping me. Here we need to use a habitual form of *cha*, *chatosh*, or alternatively *hatosh*, along with a special negator *ba*.

Kana kia't si-apela chatoshba.
No one ever helps me. (Literally, "Someone never helps me.")

Negative Emphasis: *Ke* and *kashke*

In Choctaw we may provide extra emphasis, both positive and negative, by use of particular mood markers. There are no English equivalents to these expressions. The particles *ke* and *kashke* are used along with a verb in the *ik-o* form of the negative for emphasis. Some Choctaw speakers always use *ketuk* or *ketok* when using a negative verb in the past tense.

"Sapokni ato taloat anta ka̱ ak-haklo ketok, amba svshki ato taloah billia tok." (from chapter 2, slightly respelled)
I did *not* hear Grandma sing, but my mother sang all the time.

In the example above, *ak-haklo ketok* includes the negative verb *ak-haklo* 'I didn't hear' plus another expression, *ketok*, which emphasizes the negative. The negative particle *ke* is very often attached to a tense marker. (This particle was introduced in chapter 5.)

Ik-chi-yimmo ketuk.
You did *not* believe it.

Note again that the *ke* particle is used when the verb is negated with *ik-o* rather than with the *kiyo* marker.

In contrast, the positive emphasis marker *ahe* may be used (as a verbal suffix rather than a prefix on the tense marker):

Nipi ish-chompahe tuk.
You *did* buy meat.

As we noted in chapter 8, the emphatic mood has a special negative form, *kashke*, which is used with the *ik-o* negative. Compare the following examples:

a. Nipi chik-chompo ketuk.
   You did *not* buy meat.
b. Nipi chik-chompo kashke.
   You should *not* (or do *not*) buy meat.

ANUMPA

Nouns

ashiḻa	[a-shį́-lʋ]	dry spot among wet ones
iti nakshish	[i-ti nák-shish]	tree limb; bush
kapali	[ka-pá-li]	bridle bit
kapali isht talakchi	[ka-pa-li isht ta-lák-chi]	reins

Verbs

ʋbanʋblichi	[ʋ-bʋ-nʋb-li-chi]	put over; cause to go over
afohommi	[a-fo-hum-mi]	put on a rim
akkoa, akkowa	[ak-ko-ʋ]	go down; get down; dismount
apaknakachi	[a-pak-ná-kʋ-chi]	get on top of something; go overhead
filemoa	[fi-le-mo-ʋ]	turn this way and that
wakeli	[wa-ke-li]	lift; raise up

Adverbs

chatok, chatuk	[cha-tok]	ever in the past; used to
chatok kiyo	[cha-tok ke-yu]	never in the past
chatosh	[cha-tush]	ever habitually
chatoshba	[cha-tush ba]	never habitually
makashinli	[ma-kʋ-shį-li]	the same as
tomba	[to̱-bʋ]	very
yʋmmak kia	[yʋm-mak ki-ʋ]	likewise; also

Location Words

pilla	[pil-lʋ]	from; off in distant space or time

Idioms

ahollopi ia chatuk	used to go to grave houses
ʋbanʋblichit pilla	throw over

filemoat pit pisa   look around
i̱-nowat a̱ya   visit someone (recipient object)

Anumpa Anukfilli: Verbs Compounded with Directional and Positional Particles

Choctaw has a great many verbs that are compounded with location words (just as English does) to give complex meanings. Some of these words are easy to take apart; others are more obscure.

Made from *akka* 'down'
akkoa   go down; get down
akkabohli   lay down
akkahika; akkanowa   journey on foot
akkakaha   lie down
akkakoha   fall down
akkitola   fall down

Made from *apaknaka* 'on top of'
apaknakachi   get on top of something

Made from *apakfoa* 'round'
apakfobli   go around; surround
apakshanofa   cling
apakshv̲nni   twist around

Made from *misha* 'beyond'
mishema   be beyond

Made from *v̲bana* 'lie across'
v̲banv̲blichi   leap over something

Made from *om*; o̲ 'on'
ombitepa   press on
ombalili   ride on something
ombinili   ride or sit on something
onatula   fall on

Abₐchi

Chi-anukfokah-o̲?

Look back through the story *Ahollopi* and locate all the conversations. How else could they be translated?

Anumpa ₐlhpesa

A. Write ten sentences in Choctaw using a negated noun phrase. Write five sentences that make use of *chatok kiyo* and *chatoshba*.

B. Make sentences with several of the compounded verb forms from the "Anumpa Anukfilli" section. For example: Issoba ma̲ ish-ombalili ha̲? "Aren't you riding (on) that horse?"

C. What do these sentences mean?

1. ₐlla moma kₐt pₐlhki hosh balili kia kana't ik-akkatolo ketuk.
2. Chi̲ki yₐt issuba ombinili ka̲ chim-issa chatoshba.

Holissochi

Write a short anecdote in Chahta Anumpa that includes at least one short conversation. Include a negative expression. Translate to Nahullo Anumpa.

CHAPTER 10

Holisso Atoka et Pila
'A Letter from Atoka'

Choctaw Text and Translation: *Holisso Atoka et Pila* 'A Letter from Atoka', by Rannie Winthrop

The Reverend Rainey (Rannie) Winthrop of Atoka, Oklahoma, conducted much of his pastoral care by mail. Here we have a letter dated March 20, 1885, to Alfol Folsom, who is grieving for his deceased wife. The letter has been transcribed here and is seen in the photograph in its original hand and spelling.

Mach 20, 1885
Atoka

Alfol Folsom

Anumpa iti-sa-pila toka himmaka pit chim-ᴠlachishke, yohmi ka nana nukhaklo anumpa hosh, ayat am-ᴠla cha pisa-lih mᴠt sachokᴠsh ᴠt nukhaklo aialhi tokoke. Yohmi kia nana sa-yukpa kano takalih akinli tok. ᴠbanumpa ha ishit im-ᴠlhtayyaha cha illi tok. Ilᴠppako haklo-lih mᴠt sayukpa fehna tokoke; yohmi hoka himmaka pilla ka ohoyo chiholitopa yᴠmma nashoka ya ish-pisahekeyu makoke. Amba chishno yakosh ᴠbanumpa ha ishit chim-alhtayyaha cha ish-ahanta tok pulla hosh, kanima kashinli ho ohoyo yᴠmma ahoyyochit ish-pisa, hiya. Yᴠmmᴠk illa hosh takali hoke ilᴠppakosh ayat chim-ᴠlachi kiyo—hoka. Amba chishno

98

yakosh aia̱lhit maha̱yat ish-moma hok makosh ish-pisahinla; yᴠmmᴠk illa hoke yakni inla pila ᴠba yakni yᴠmmano a̱yat iti̱fillᴠmmahekeyu yᴠmma okᴠt abilia.

Yohmi makoke yohmi hoka̱ anukfillit ish-pihi̱sashke.

Pi̱chukka lokoli maya kᴠt achukma mayahoke; yohmik ma̱ ᴠno yᴠt am-achukma kiyoh fehna momah akinli hoke. Chukkachᴠffa i̱maya kᴠt abikfih mᴠt ilaiasha billia hoke.

Mach nittak 22 yᴠmma chukka lokoli ilᴠppa itihalᴠllachi̱ am-anoa tokosh ia-lachi̱ hoke. Pissatabbi yakosh ohoyo halᴠllachi̱ , miya hoke.

Anumpa kᴠllo imma, is-samichike
Rev. Rannie Winthrop

March 20, 1885
Atoka

Alfol Folsom

You'll be receiving my correspondence right away; so it is the sad news has come to me, and when I viewed it my heart was truly sad. Nevertheless, there is happiness that can be had here.

She had received the Gospel before she died. When I heard this I was very happy indeed. And so it is that from now on you will not ever be able to see your dearest spouse's face. But you, after having received the Gospel, must continue to live; sometime it may be permitted to find and see that spouse—perhaps. That is the only way because she won't come to you herself. And you, if you still continue on truly, you will be able to see this. That other world, heaven, in going there you will never be parted ever.

This is the way it is, and you should continue to study it.

Our neighborhood continues to do well. But as for me, I'm still not very well. Our family who are here are very sickly, as always.

I was told that on March 22 there will be a wedding in our neighborhood; I'm definitely going. Pissatabbi, they say, will marry some woman.

You bid me speak firm words [a formal closing],
Rev. Rannie Winthrop

English translation by Henry Willis and Marcia Haag

This is June 11th 1900
monday.

Mach 20 1885
atoka

Alfol Folsom
Anumpa iti sam pilo
Toka himka pit etim
ali chishki Yoh mika
Nano nok haklo anumpa
hosh anyot amali cha
pisali mot sachokash ot
nok haklo ayanhli tok oki
yohmikia nana sayokpa
kano takalli hakinli tok
Abbanumpa ha ishit
Omahl taya hacha illi tok
illoppako hakloli mot
Sayokpafihma tok oki
yohmi hoka himolla pili
ka ohoyo chi holitopa
yamma nashoka ya ish
pisa li kiyohmakoke

These photographs of Reverend Rannie Winthrop's pastoral letter to Alfol Folsom show the choices of spelling and word divisions that the Reverend used in his writing. *Courtesy of the Western History Collections, University of Oklahoma.*

Amba chish no
yakosh abbanumpa ka
ishit chimahl tay a hacha
isha hanta tok pollo
hosh kanna kashunlli
ho ohayo yamma ahayo
chit ishpisa hiya
yamak illo hosh tokali
hoki ilvp akosh anyot
chimalo chi kiyo — hoka
Amba chish no yakosh
ayanhlit ma hanyat ishi
monna hok makosh ish
pisa hinlo yamak ilo
hoki yakni inlo pilo
aba yakni yammano
Ayit tipillin ann hin kiyo
yamma okot ahilia
yakni makoki
johni hoka anokfillit
ish pi hinsash ki

Omi chuka
lokoli maya kut
Achok ma maya hoki
yohmik ma ano yut
amachuk ma kiyoh fih
na moma hakinli hoki
chuka achaffa imaya
kut abikfihnt
iluyasha billia hoki
        Mach nitok 22
yamma chuka lokoli
iluppa it tchalali chi
amanow a tokosh iyalu
chi hoki Pissatabbi
yakosh ahoyo hallo
    chi mia hoki

            Amunpa Hallo
                imma
        issamchik i
Rev Ramie Winthrop

ANUMPA ѴLHPESA: Complex Predicates

Complex predicates—those made with the -t form—are one of the most prevalent and important Choctaw predicate forms. We have already studied their basic uses (see chapter 12 in *Choctaw Language and Culture*). Here we have a more extensive overview of the kinds of complex predicates that Choctaw uses, divided into four basic types. The student may find that these divisions make the -t forms easier to understand.

Putting Predicates Together

Let's review the way complex predicates are formed.

1. Complex predicates always share the same subject.
The main predicate, the last one, is the one that bears the subject marker, if there is one, and the tense and mood markers, if there are any. The secondary predicates are marked with -t.

"Yohmi makoke yohmi hoka anukfillit ish-pihisashke."
This is the way it is and so you should continue to study it.

In the example above, the main predicate, the verb *pisa*, is marked for the iterative aspect and the emphatic mood to form *pihisashke*. It carries the person marker *ish-*. The secondary predicate, *anukfilli*, is marked with -t. It has the same subject and tense as *pisa*. *Pihisa* means 'pore over' and *anukfulli* means 'think'. As a complex predicate it means 'to look carefully at something while thinking about it', or 'to study it'.

2. A secondary predicate may have its own objects and object markers.

"Ikana ya i-nowat aya tok, miya" (from chapter 9).
He said he was visiting his friend.

In the above example, the secondary predicate *nowat* 'walk' has an object marker *i-*, which refers to its object, 'his friend'. The main predicate, *aya* 'travel', appears before the tense marker, *tok*. The complex predicate *i-nowat aya* means 'travel by walking to someone' and is a way of expressing 'visit'.

". . . okti m̲a bolit chiluk ish-ikbik mʋt . . ." (from chapter 22, *Choctaw Language and Culture*)
. . . if you pound the ice and make a hole . . .

In the example above, the secondary predicate, the verb *bolit* 'pound', has its own object, *okti m̲a* 'the/that ice'. The main predicate, the verb *ikbi* 'make', also has its own object, *chiluk* 'hole' and also carries the person marker and tense marker.

3. Secondary predicates may carry aspect markers, but aspect is much more commonly marked on the main predicate.

"Itikba ma, taloh̲owat, ilbʋshat kiloh-aiasha." (ʋba isht taloa #74, *Choctaw Hymn Book*)
Let us all be there ahead, humbly, singing on and on.

In the example above, the secondary predicate *taloh̲owat* 'sing on and on' is marked for iterative aspect (it is based on *taloa*). Notice that in the example in section 1. above, the iterative aspect was marked only on the main predicate, but its meaning was carried through the entire sentence.

Uses of Complex Predicates

There are four distinct ways that complex predicates are used. These can be hard to distinguish and keep straight. We will often need to think about the word meanings before translating them to English, which has its own several ways of doing the same things.

Serial phrases

The first use for complex predicates is simply putting together a series of phrases that have the same subject and tense. These sentences can be easily translated with a conjunction like *and.*

". . . s̲iti y̲o pisah mʋt itakha isht pit lhachakat ishit halat kuchi cha koblit ʋbih mʋt fol̲otat sabbʋk ant holakshit . . ." (from chapter 24, *Choctaw Language and Culture*)
. . . [S]he saw the snake and then she snatched it with her mouth, and took it outside and so she bit it and killed it and then returned and came and licked my hand . . .

In the example above, there are three forms of conjunction: *mvt*, *cha*, and *-t*. These do very much the same work: they put the events in a sequence. The *-t* forms are the most neutral, in that they do not include the sense of 'then' (*mvt*) or 'so' (*cha*).

"Shokvta hasimbish vt tohbit wanukshot pisachukmah bieka tok" (from chapter 21, *Choctaw Language and Culture*).
The opossum's tail used to be white, fluffy, and beautiful.

In this example, the *-t* forms put the predicates *tohbi* 'white' and *wanuksho* 'fluffy' in a series with *pisachukma* 'beautiful'.

Purpose and outcome
Another use for complex predicates is to state purpose or outcome. These may be translated with *to* or with the *-ing* form (the present participle) in English. Remember that in Choctaw, the main verb will come last, and the purpose or outcome clause will be marked with *-t*. This use is particularly common with verbs of motion, such as *ia*, or with verbs such as *tahli*.

a. Aiitatoba ya sholush himona chompat il-iachi.
We're going to the store to buy new shoes.
b. "Aki yvt toksvlit iak mvt holissopisa shali aiyokopa yo ontsa-kanchi . . ." (from chapter 1)
When my father went to work he left me at the bus stop. (Here *toksvlit iak* means that he went somewhere for the purpose of working.)
c. Taloat ish-yokopa.
You stopped to sing. (*Not* "You stopped singing." That would be *Taloa kvt ish-yokopa*.)
d. ". . . chekossi ho apoksiat tahli tuk" (from chapter 16, *Choctaw Language and Culture*).
After a while he finished repairing it.

The forms *V-t pisa* 'try to' and *V-t ishtia* 'start to' are of this type:

a. Nvni lvwa ka yokachit pisa-li tuk.
I tried to catch a lot of the fish.

b. ". . . svshki tapushik ikbi im-aiikhanat ishtia-li tok" (from chapter 2).
I started to learn basket making from my mother.

Modifying predicates

A third very important use for complex predicates is to use one predicate, the one marked with -*t*, to modify the main predicate, the one that
comes last:

a. ". . . mak fokali ma shali okhisushi lhipullichit pit e-pisah ma,
chanvlli yvt hina chanvllit aya tok" (from chapter 6).
About that time we looked out the car window and a tire was
rolling down the road. (Here *chanvllit aya* literally means 'moving
along rolling'.)
b. ". . . svllahachih ma, ashaka vlhi yvt akkitolat tvli pvtha isso mah,
kanima moma luak polohlichit pila tok" (from chapter 6).
When she slowed down, the rear end hit down on the pavement
and sent sparks flying everywhere.

In example a., *akkitolat* 'land down' modifies *isso* 'hit', and *polohlichit*
'make spark' modifies *pila* 'send'. Remember that we must put the literal
meanings into something that sounds natural in English!

Idioms

Another very large group of complex predicates is made up of forms
that have been reduced from other words or are completely idiomatic.
Some of the reduced forms are *pit*, from *pilat; ant* from *alat; ont*, from
onat, and *momint*, from *momichit*.

a. Takkon momint vpa tuk.
He ate up the peach.
b. Holisso pit ish-pila.
You're sending a letter (away from yourself).

Other idiomatic and very common complex predicates are:

vttat aya 'going along'
Hattak vt nowat vttat aya.
The man was walking along.

(Verb)-*t kạchi* 'do something to an extreme'
". . . ibbvk pahta bvshlit kạchi tok." (from chapter 23, *Choctaw Language and Culture*)
. . . he cut his palm badly.

(Verb)-*t kania* 'do or be something all the way'
"Atukọ shukvta yvt yimmitat kania hosh . . ." (from chapter 21, *Choctaw Language and Culture*)
And so it was that the opossum, all excited . . .

Kvt and *-t*

One of the hardest intuitions for the English speaker to gain is the difference between *kvt* and *-t*. In general the difference is that *-t* forms mark predicates that are interpreted as part of the same event, either as a series or as a manner. *Kvt* marks *complements*, to use the grammatical term. This means that they are the object of the main verb. Another way to think about this is that complements answer the question What? But these are not always straightforward: each language has certain expressions that seem to break the rules and will have to be learned one by one.

Okshinilli kvt ish-aiokpạchi-hạ?
You enjoy swimming, don't you?

In the example above, we use *kvt* because swimming is the *thing* that is enjoyed, it is not the *way* it is enjoyed. *Swimming* is the object of the main verb *enjoy*.

Nakfish vt okshinillit ia tuk.
My little brother/sister went swimming.

In this example, swimming is part of the event—going and swimming—so we use *-t*.

a. Toksali kvt issa-li.
   I quit working. (*Not* "I quit to work.")
b. Toksalit ishtia-li.
   I began to work.

In Choctaw, 'start to' or 'begin to' takes the *-t* marker; it is considered part of the event. But 'stop' takes *kʋt*; what is stopped is considered the object of the verb.

ANUMPA

Nouns

chukka lokoli	[chuk-kʋ lu-kó-li]	neighborhood
itombi	[i-tó̠-bi]	box; square container

Verbs

alotali	[a-lo-tʋ-li]	pack; load
ashachi	[a-sha-chi]	store; put away
halʋlli	[ha-lʋl-li]	draw together; marry
ipota	[i̠-pu-tʋ]	lend to someone (recipient object)
iti̠filʋmmi	[i-ti fi-lʋm-mi]	part from each other
itihalʋlli	[i-ti-ha-lʋl-li]	get married
lokoli, lukoli	[lu-ko-li]	cluster or group together
takali	[tʋ-ka-li]	be; hang

Adjectives

takali	[ta-ká-li]	connected

Adverbs

abilia	[a-bi-li-ʋ]	always
himmaka pilla	[him-ma-ka pil-lʋ]	from now on
kanima kashinli	[k-ni-mʋa kash i̠-li]	sometime

Idioms

ʋbanumpa ishit im-ʋlhtaha		receive the Gospel
anumpa iti-pila		correspondence
hiya	[he-ya]	perhaps

ANUMPA ANUKFILLI: Compound Verbs

One common use of complex predicates is to join them to make verbs or other predicates, such as adjectives, with richer meanings. We always use the -t form to do this. We do not put two verbs together in the English manner.

Notice how these complex, or compound, verbs are made up of a main predicate and a modifying one:

ikhanachit pehlichi	teach + lead	discipline
ilefehnachit nowa	proud + walk	strut
yichiffit ishi	grasp + hold	seize
nukshopat wvnnichi	afraid + shake	tremble with fear
chitolit fiopa	do hard + breathe	sigh
achukmalit pisa	do well + look	scrutinize
kuchit ashachi	take out + put away	unload

Abvchi

Chi-anukfokah-o?

Examine Reverend Winthrop's letter again, paying attention to the number of emphatic markers (*oke* and *shke*) that he uses. How else might these be translated?

Anumpa vlhpesa

A. Uses of complex predicates

1. Write four sentences using complex predicates that form serial phrases.
2. Write another four sentences using complex predicates that indicate purpose or outcome.
3. Write another four sentences using complex predicates where one modifies another.
4. Use four different idiomatic -t forms in sentences.

B. *kvt* versus -t: Translate the following sentences to Choctaw, choosing the correct connector.

1. I like to eat squash.
2. Some man came to help us.
3. You're skillful at dancing.
4. We stopped to eat dinner.
5. We stopped eating.
6. My teacher was totally angry.
7. Our neighbor tried to make us angry.
8. I forgot to wash the dishes.
9. My little brother sat quietly.
10. The men harvested the corn, hauled it to the barn, and unloaded it.

C. What is the difference in the meanings of these sentences?

1. Hattak micha imohoyo ahinna mʋt itihalʋllit pisa tuk.
2. Hattak micha imohoyo ahinna mʋt itihalʋlli kʋt im-ahoba tuk.

Holissochi

Write a letter in Choctaw to a friend. Include several complex predicates and several emphatic pronouns and emphatic markers.

CHAPTER 11

"Iti Hishi Yvmma
Isht Chi'thaiyana-li Hoke"
'A Leaf that Reminds Me of Thee'

Choctaw Text and Translation: "Iti Hishi Yvmma Isht Chi'thaiyana-li
Hoke" 'A Leaf that Reminds Me of Thee', by William H. McKinney

*This is the first known poem in the Choctaw language, written by
William H. McKinney in 1878. The reader will notice that the theme and
flowery language are representative of the poetic style of nineteenth-century
English literature. The reader of the Choctaw language will also notice
that the Choctaw itself is quite straightforward in its style—a good lesson
in how much freedom the translator has.*

I

Hvshi kanvlli achukma il-ima ka
    Nowat aya kvt yoka keyu hosh chianukfihillit,
Ikana yvt anta ka ikhaiyanak mvt:
    Chishno ma isht ikhaiyana-li hoke!
Yohmi ka isanahchi yvt pvchi yoshoba holba hosh
    Peni akohchat sachokvsh vt mahli okpulo
Okhata itvnnvp a cholusa ha falamichit ishtvlak ma
    Iti hishi yvmma isht chi'thaiyana-li hoke.

II

Yohmi ka shutik vt oklhilikak ma,
    Oka yvt hofobi micha pvtha moma ka,

Nanishtikana yvt okhata lapalika ya onitolat
  Tikba pilla hopaki kia kaniohmi tukvt
Imomaka fochik a ish-pisa ka
  Sachokvsh ashosh chi-anukfihili tukvt
Kanima ont issahekeyu hoke.

III

Yohmi ka Chikana ya pisa-li kvt
  chihochifo ma haklo li aiena kia kaniohmit atuk
Olvllahekeyuk mvt nana nukhaklo yvt,
  vlak ma yakni ilvppak ash
Nana makaniohmi ya ithana;
  Yohmi cha okhina bachoha puta ka
ithana kia ahofobi ont ia yvmmano keyu tokoke.

I

How Sweet is the hour we give,
  When fancy may wander free,
To the friends who in memory live! —
  For then I remember thee!
Then, winged, like the dove from the ark
  My heart, o'er a stormy sea,
Brings back to my lonely bark
  A leaf that reminds me of thee!

II

But still does the sky look dark,
  The waters still deep and wide,
Oh: when may my lonely bark
  In peace on the shore abide?
But through the future far,
  Dark though my course may be,
Thou art my guiding Star!
  My heart still turns to thee:

III

When I see thy friends I smile,
  I sigh when I hear thy name;

But they cannot tell the while
   Whence the smile or the sadness came,
Vainly the world may deem
   The cause of my sighs they know:
The breeze that ruffles the stream
   Knows not the depth below.

                Choctaw and English by William H. McKinney,
                        transliterated by the authors

ANUMPA VLHPESA: Definiteness

Although there is nothing more natural in our language than using words like *a* and *the*, the system of definiteness is actually one of the most complicated and hard to explain. Perhaps you have an acquaintance from another country who seems to never quite master when to use *a* and when to use *the*. You know exactly the right way to use these words, but you will have a great deal of trouble explaining what you know if you try to help.

The Choctaw system of definiteness is much larger and more complicated than that in English. We have already been introduced to a large number of the particles that belong to the definiteness system. These include all the subject and object markers (such as *at, hosh, a,* and *o̱*), the demonstratives (such as *yvmma*), the contrast markers (such as *-ato*), and the focus markers (such as *akosh*).

What Is Definiteness?

Whenever we talk about a thing, or, speaking grammatically, when we use a noun phrase, we must communicate something about how specific that thing is. Sometimes we wish to pick out something from a group. Other times we wish to introduce something for the first time. Then we may wish to refer to something that has already been introduced. Or we may wish to talk about something in general terms, without a specific reference in mind. Most languages accomplish this with sets of particles that identify how definite, indefinite, specific, or general something is.

Introducing Information

One important task for the definiteness system is to introduce new information. In English, we frequently will use the article *a* to mark such a noun phrase if it is singular, and use no marking if it is plural.

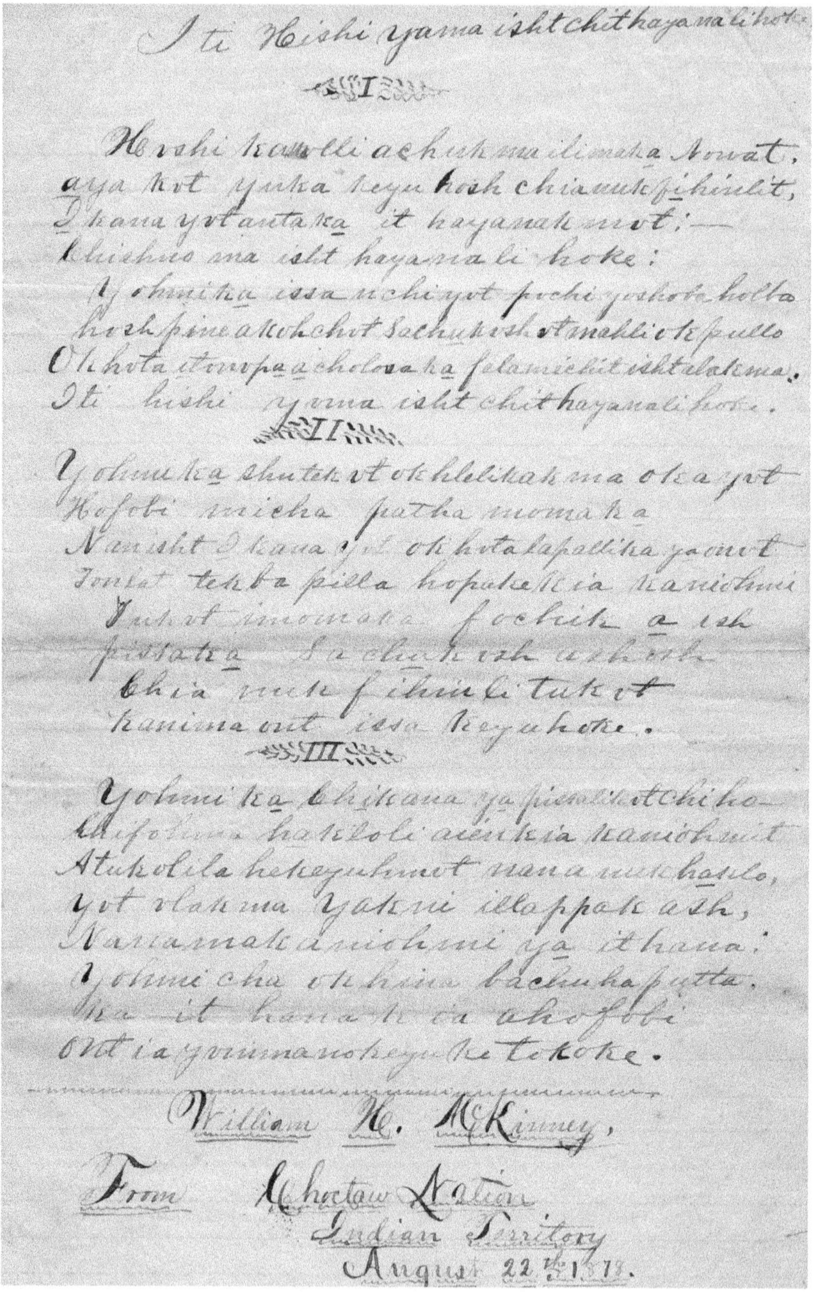

Iti Hishi yama isht chithayanali hoke

❦ I ❦

[handwritten Choctaw verse — six lines]

❦ II ❦

[handwritten Choctaw verse]

❦ III ❦

[handwritten Choctaw verse]

William H. McKinney,

From Choctaw Nation
Indian Territory
August 22ᵈ 1878.

William McKinney's poem, which he wrote in both Choctaw and English, appears on lined paper in his own hand. Note the hand-drawn filigree and other embellishments, and the style of penmenship. *Courtesy of the Western History Collections, University of Oklahoma.*

A leaf that Reminds me of thee —

I

How sweet is the hour we give,
  When fancy may wander free,
To the friends who in memory live! —
  For then I remember thee!
Then, winged, like the dove from the ark,
  My heart, o'er a stormy sea,
Bring back to my lonely bark
  A leaf that reminds me of thee!

II

But still does the sky look dark,
  The waters still deep and wide,
Oh: when may my lonely bark
  In peace on the shore abide?
But through the future far,
  Dark though my course may be,
Thou art my guiding Star!
  My heart still turns to thee:

III

When I see thy friends I smile,
  I sigh when I hear thy name;
But they cannot tell the while
  Whence the smile or the sadness came;
Vainly the world may deem
  The cause of my sighs they know:
The breeze that ruffles the stream
  Knows not the depth below.

115

Did you see a white cat?
There's a big, hungry opossum outside the door!
Three strange men just showed up.

Notice how the speaker recognizes in the examples above that the listener has not yet identified what the topic of conversation is. If we change the article to *the* in these sentences, their meaning changes completely:

Did you see the white cat?
There's the big, hungry opossum outside the door!
The three strange men just showed up.

In these sentences, the speaker assumes that the listener already knows about the white cat, the big, hungry opossum, and the three strange men. The use of *the* lets us know that the information has already been introduced.

In Choctaw, when we introduce information, we may leave the noun phrase unmarked if it is not a subject, and we very often use the *osh* subject marker if it is a subject:

a. Katos tohbi ish-pisa ha?
   Did you see a white cat?
b. Shukhata hohchvffo chito yosh kucha yvmma anta.
   There's a big, hungry opossum outside.

In example b., *yosh* tells the listener that some opossum, not yet identified, has become the topic of conversation.

c. Hattak nukshobahinla tuchina hosh haiahka.
   Three scary men just showed up.

In example c. above, the subject marker *hosh* is used to indicate that the listener doesn't know about the three scary men.

Referring to Information Already Introduced

Once a topic has been introduced, it can be referred to because it is definite. Both English and Choctaw have markers to refer to noun phrases already introduced. In English, we generally use *the*, but we may also use the demonstratives *this, that, these,* and *those* to do so, or in very formal speech or writing, *the latter, the former, the aforementioned,* and a few others.

> 1a. There's an opossum outside. This opossum looks particularly hungry.
> 1b. There's an opossum outside. An opossum looks particularly hungry.
> 2a. Three strange men showed up. No one knows the men.
> 2b. Three strange men showed up. No one knows three strange men.

As the sentences above illustrate, once the topic has been introduced, it must take a *definite* reference to be interpreted as the same thing the next time it is mentioned. Notice how odd the sentences are that fail to do so: they suggest that we are introducing another topic.

In Choctaw, we have far more markers to refer back to an already introduced noun phrase. Each of these markers adds a bit of information or suggests a slightly different context.

Ash

One very strong marker, which always means 'the aforementioned', is *ash*, which is also seen in its variant form *yash*. This marker is attached at the end of the noun phrase (as are all such markers) and gives a strong reference to the topic under discussion. It is very useful in telling stories and anecdotes, when we need to track topics through the discourse. It also is used when we just want someone to know we are referring to a previously mentioned thing or person. We attach a subject marker, *-ot* or *-osh*, when the noun phrase is a subject, and we may also attach *-o̱* when it is an object. We may also attach any of the contrast markers, or focus markers, to make very specific references; these are not easily translated to English since English lacks this large array of particles.

> a. "Ahma shawi ashot, to̱shpat nana ᵥpahinla kᵥt . . ." (from chapter 21, *Choctaw Language and Culture*)
> And so that raccoon, who wanted to hurry to find something to eat . . .
> b. "Hattak ashosh nana kaniomahinla kᵥt ik-ikhano kia anukfillit tahlih mᵥt . . ." (from chapter 23, *Choctaw Language and Culture*)
> The man did not know what to do, but he thought about it and then . . .

In examples a. and b. we are telling stories in which a raccoon and a man are characters. We use *ashot* in one sentence and *ashosh* in the other to indicate that it's the same raccoon and man we have been talking about all along. It is very difficult to distinguish *ashot* from *ashosh* in English translation; they will inevitably be translated the same way. However, in storytelling, *ashosh* will be used the first time the character is referred to, and *ashot* for subsequent referrals:

> a. Hattak ashosh miti.
>   The (known) man is coming.
> b. Hattak ashot miti.
>   The same known man is coming.

The object form of *ash/yash* is *asho/yasho*. This form is used when the noun phrase is not a subject:

> a. Ofi yasho pisa-li.
>   I see the dog (the one referred to).

We can take advantage of this particle to get the sense of the English phrases 'the one that' or 'the one who'.

> b. Anumpuli yasho ish-pisa ha?
>   Did you (or do you) see the one who spoke?
> c. Anumpuli yashosh ilvppa anta.
>   The one who spoke is here.

Another form of *ash* is *chash*. The compound form *osh chash* is often use to refer to the deceased. It can also be used to mean 'former':

> a. Sapokni osh chash Missippi ahanta tok.
>   My late Grandmother lived in Mississippi.
> b. Holisso satibapishi osh chash a-nowat aya tok.
>   My former schoolmate visited me.

Kash

We see *ash* in the form of *kash* when it is attached to predicates. *Kash* has two important uses. One of its uses is to refer to past time, or to an event that was referred to previously:

"Hopak kash o nowvt ayvt chukka ant chukkovt binili makinli ho . . ." (from chapter 2). *Note also this variation:* "Hopakikash ano nowat aya´t chukka ant chukkoat binili makinli ho . . ."
A long time ago, as soon as a visitor came in the house and sat down . . .

A second important use of *kash* is to describe nouns, using a clause. In English, we use relative clauses to do this. Such descriptive clauses marked with *kash* may be translated as relative clauses. Recall that in Choctaw we have a more familiar way to do this, using *kvt* and *ka*.

 a. Hattak binili kash kania tuk.
    The man who was sitting there went away.
 b. Hattak ia kash ish-pisa ha?
    Did you see the man who left?

Compare these forms to the way we have made such clauses previously (see chapter 22, *Choctaw Language and Culture*):

 a. Hattak binili tukvt kania tuk.
    The man who was sitting there went away.
 b. Hattak ia tuka ish-pisa ha?
    Did you see the man who left?

In the first set of examples, *kash* points out the man we are talking about. This particle may appear in both the subject and the object—it does not need to track the subject the way other Choctaw particles do.

Generic or Nonspecific Items

Sometimes we want to talk about something in a general way or have in mind a kind of thing, but not a specific item—in other words, something that has no reference in the discourse.

Do you know where I can buy a newspaper?
We don't sell bread.
Books are sold over there.

In these English sentences, we may use the indefinite article *a* if the thing is countable, no marker if the thing is a *mass noun*, or not countable (like bread), or the plural form.

In Choctaw, we similarly use no marker for things that are nonspecific. But as soon as we pick out something specific about an item, we use a focus marker or definite article. We do this much more readily in Choctaw than in English.

> a. Palvska e-kanchi kiyo.
>   We don't sell bread.
> b. Palvska nanta ohmi ako chi-bvnnah-o?
>   What kind of bread do you want?
> c. Tanch palvska ako sa-bvnna.
>   I want cornbread. (Literally, "It's cornbread I want.")

In example a., we are simply making a nonspecific reference to bread. But in b., we focus on a particular kind of bread, which calls for the focus marker *ako*. Then in example c., we focus again on the type of bread, cornbread, so again we use *ako* to specify the type.

In these examples, we have already been talking about bread, and so when we focus on a particular kind of bread, cornbread, in Choctaw we need to show that these two ideas are related by using a focus marker. In English, we just assume we are talking about the same topic.

This difference shows up frequently in English expressions that are specific but have not been introduced yet. Such expressions will most often not take the definite article *the*. But in Choctaw these must take a definiteness marker because they are narrowing down the description of something. Notice how the two languages treat the information in the following pairs of sentences:

> The raccoon is an animal that lives in the forest.
> A raccoon is an animal that lives in the forest.
> Raccoons are animals that live in the forest.
> Shawi ato napoa nukshopa kowi anuka ako asha.

These sentences give us a definition of *raccoon*. English may use a variety of ways to express this, but Choctaw simply uses *ato*, the contrastive subject marker that tells the listener that the raccoon is to be distinguished from other things. English does not have such a marker. Notice also that Choctaw uses the definite focus marker *-ako* to point out 'in the forest'. Both languages note that 'an animal' is indefinite. English uses the indefinite article *an* to mark it, and Choctaw does not mark *napoa nukshopa*.

I am looking for a book about the Choctaw language.
Holisso hʋt Chahta Anumpa imma yo̱ hoyo-li.

In the example above, we again have an item that has not been introduced but is specific: a book, but a certain kind of book. In Choctaw, the fact that we have narrowed down the kind of book (as we narrowed down the kind of bread in the earlier example) requires some kind of marking to point this out. In this case, the adverbial clause marker -*yo̱* has been used, which gives the sentence a literal meaning something like: "I'm looking for a book, which is about the Choctaw language."

I'm looking for the perfect man.
Hattak a̱lhi yo̱ hoyo-li.

In this example, English uses an idiomatic expression, 'the perfect man', to indicate a type, similar to 'the raccoon' above. Choctaw again uses -*yo̱* in an expression that translates "I'm looking for a man who is true."

Marked Indefinites

Sometimes we want to positively mark something as being indefinite. In both English and Choctaw we have indefinite pronouns, modifiers, and adverbials that will do this for us.

Some man came looking for you.
Hattak nana hosh chi-hoyot a̱ya tuk.

In this example, both Choctaw and English use an indefinite modifier, *nana* 'some', to positively state that the man has no description and has not been introduced in discourse. Notice that Choctaw uses the subject marker *hosh* to indicate this fact, as explained earlier.

Recall the set of Choctaw indefinites. When these are used in the subject, we will use *hosh* to mark the subject rather than a form of *ʋt*. *Ho̱* or another focus marker is frequently used to set off the indefinite expression:

a. Kanimma il-ilhkoli. (Often *kanimma ak̠o*)
   We're going somewhere.
b. Nana il-akostinichi tuk.
   We found out something.
c. Kana hosh haiaka tuk.
   Somebody showed up.
d. Kaniohmi h̠o il-ayona tuk.
   We got there somehow.
e. Kana kia hosh pi-apelach̠i.
   Someone or other will help us.
f. vlla kanima hosh awashoha.
   Some child is playing there.
g. "Kanima moma luak polohlichit pila tok" (from chapter 6).
   They sent sparks flying everywhere.

Compounded Focus, Contrast, and Definiteness Markers

The discovery of the huge array of focus, contrast, and definiteness markers in Choctaw tends to unsettle even the most dedicated student. We know already that English does not have the equipment to make the kinds of distinctions in the grammar that Choctaw does, so we have to instead learn the general meanings of the markers so that we can make an intelligent translation. Many times we will have to translate different Choctaw expressions using the same English.

Ak and Its Classmates: Putting Something into Focus

The *ak* group of markers serves to pick things out, make them definite, put them into focus, make them distinct, and contrast them with other things. Each subject-marked form has a nonsubject form paired with it. Here are examples of the class of definiteness markers. Notice the effect they have on the way we are to interpret the information in the sentence.

ak

This particle makes something distinct. It is always compounded with another contrast or focus marker, very often *osh/o̠* or *ato/ano*. We may also see *ak* compounded with *ok* to may *akokano, akokat,* or *akokato.* It often appears with the demonstratives to make *mak* and *pak*, which are similarly compounded.

a. Chukka asha vt hoshotika ako abinohli.
   The family is seated on the porch. (*ak* + focus marker; picks out the porch as a distinct place)
b. Chukka itabana akano aiokpachi-li.
   I like the *log house*. (*ak* + contrast marker; contrasts the log house with others)
c. Apolusli makato okpulot taha.
   That tire is completely bad. (demonstrative + *ak* + contrastive subject; picks out the tire and contrasts it with other tires)

ok

This particle is used like *ak*. It is usually compounded with contrast markers and also with *ak*. Expressions made with *ok* and *ak* compounds are not easily distinguished in English, but *ok* is a stronger indication of contrast.

a. Nittak okano vla-lachi.
   On that day I will arrive. (*ok* + contrastive marker; picks out "that day" as contrasted with any other)
b. Ohoyo mato Akinsa aivlhpa kia hattak okmakato ilvppa aivlhpa tok.
   That woman was born in Arkansas, but that other man was born here. (*ok* + *mak* + contrastive marker; shows distinction between the two persons.)

The definite particles can be attached to verbs and other predicates in Choctaw, which is completely different from English, with the use of the predication marker -*h*. There is no one, good way to translate these constructions; often they can be translated with *but*.

a. "Ilvppa hikiat ia hokano / chishno akbano hosh ish-nohowa makachi pulla" (from chapter 5).
   From here on you shall have to walk alone. (The idiom 'from here on' is marked with *hokano* to point it out.)
b. "Hvklo-li hokakosh, ak-ibatalowo ketok" (from chapter 2).
   I listened but I didn't sing along.

When you read the Choctaw Bible or look through Byington's dictionary, you will often see compounded definiteness markers. If you are aware of the basic meanings of these markers, you will be more at ease in treating them simply as a way to point out something, rather than trying to analyze them one by one.

   a. "Mihma **yʋmmak ash osh** aboha ont chukowa ma . . ." (Malhu
     9:28)
     "And when **he** [the one being discussed] entered the room . . ." *or*
     ". . . and when he was come into the house . . ." (King James Bible)
   b. ". . . ohoyo himita **yash osh** tani tok" (Malhu 9:25).
     ". . . **that** young woman (the one being discussed) arose." *or* ". . .
     and the maid arose" (King James Bible).
   c. "Moses **ak okano** Chihowa yʋt im-anumpuli beka tokạ il-ithana"
     (Chan 9: 29).
     "We know that Moses **was the one whom** Jehova used to speak to."
     or "We know that God spake unto Moses . . ." (King James Bible)

ANUMPA

Nouns

fochik (variant of *fichik*)	[fú-chik]	star
imomaka	[i-mó-mʋ-ka]	experience
nanishtịkana	[na-nisht-ị-kánʋ]	peace
pʋchi yoshoba	[pʋ-chi yo-shó-bʋ]	dove

Verbs

alhowʋlit yukpạchi	[a-lho-wʋ-lit yuk-pạ-chi]	entertain; joke
akohcha	[a-koh-chʋ]	come out of; escape
bachoha (plural of bachaya)	[bʋ-cho-hʋ]	lie in rows or lanes
im-pussi	[ị-pus-si]	kiss (recipient object)
okchilhont pisa	[ok-chi-lhọt pi-sʋ]	stare at
olʋlli	[o-lʋl-li]	laugh at; mock
onochi	[o-nu-chi]	blame

Adjectives

lʋpa	[lʋ-pʋ]	blind
pʋtha	[pʋt-hʋ]	wide

Idioms

ʋlhpesat pisa	respect
anumpulit chok<u>ʋ</u>sh hotopali	insult
imomika fochik	guiding star
nukh<u>a</u>klot anoli	apologize

ANUMPA ANUKFILLI: *Pisa*

There are few words in the Choctaw language that have a bigger range of meanings than does *pisa*. Its simplest meanings are 'look' and 'see', but from here the word takes on dozens of extensions: it is used for all types of perception; for detection and scrutiny; for attempt; for examination, inspection, and investigation; and for testing and exploring.

Just as important are three variations of *pisa: apisa* (more often spelled *apesa*), *ʋlhpesa,* and *apissa.* Each of these has its own large range of meanings.

Apesa has the meanings of 'judge', 'supervise', 'order', 'resolve', 'rule', 'mediate', 'command', 'appoint', 'contract', and other words with the general sense of 'do lawfully or correctly'.

ʋlhpesa is the past participle of *apesa* and has the general meaning of the English phrase 'done correctly'. It is used for expressions that have to do with being 'all right', 'correct', 'suitable', 'proper', and 'enough'.

apissa is the form that refers to 'being straight' and is used for expressions that treat the notions of being 'direct', literally and figuratively 'straight', 'genuine', and 'true'.

All of these forms regularly enter into compounds with *-t* predicates and into word formation processes, such as the *-chi* causative marker.

ABʋCHI

Chi-anukf<u>o</u>kah-<u>o</u>?

Compare the English and Choctaw versions of Mr. McKinney's poem. Notice the poet's use of words such as 'bark' for *peni* and 'thee' for *chishno.* Make a list of words that have an antiquated style in English but are still perfectly common in Choctaw. Then note the lines or words that appear in English but not in Choctaw: what do you think the author's goal was in each language?

Anumpa vlhpesa

A. Take a noun phrase in a simple sentence and change the definiteness in Choctaw using the various particles that signify definiteness. Make at least five distinctions. Translate to Nahullo Anumpa as accurately as possible. Note how the Choctaw system, being more detailed than the English, gives a larger range of possibilities. Examples: Katos tohbi pisa-li. 'I see a white cat.' Katos tohbi ako pisa-li. 'It's the white cat I see.' and so forth.

B. Write five sentences in Chahta Anumpa using the contrastive markers *ato* and *ano* and their variations. Translate to Nahullo Anumpa. There is more than one correct way to do so.

C. What do these sentences mean?

1. Nanishtikana ako sa-bvnnashke.
2. Ohoyo kana hosh a-pussit pisa tuk.
3. Pvchi yoshoba makato vlhpichik ilvppako ikbi tuk.

Holissochi

Write a poem in Chahta Anumpa of five to ten lines. Translate it in two ways: first use common English and then use a literary or elevated style. Why are both ways correct?

CHAPTER 12

Lady, Ofi Nafehna
'Lady, the Remarkable Dog'

Choctaw Text and Translation: *Lady, Ofi Nafehna* 'Lady, the Remarkable Dog', by Henry Willis

We were introduced to Lady, the author's mongrel pet who saved him from a snake, in the first volume of Chahta Anumpa. *Here Mr. Willis tells more about this remarkable dog and their adventures together when he was a child in central Oklahoma.*

Chuka pota yvt, chuka pimapotat asha tukvt, oklah awiha mah, Lady vt makinli anta tokọ am-anoa tok. Tofa ont taha fokalih ma̲ chuka ma̲ wihat e-chukoa tok.

Tikba hvshi achvffa fokali ka̲, amafo anọti sapokni yvt Missippi iti-achih mvt Lady ya̲ iti chvnaha potalhpo nuta ponolakvllopvna isht atak-chit ilauet isht ia tok. Okhapa Yakni (Akinsa) kanima fohka ponolakvllo shvna ash akoblit itakkoluffi cha Okhapa Yakni a hopaki họ fullokachit a̲yat Okhapa Okhina akanimit lhipulli mvt, Oklahumma Yakni, a hopaki fehna họ, a̲yat chuka falamat vla tok. Ponolakvllo yushkololi yvt ikonla atalakchi moma họ nayukpa hosh wanuta ant chukoa tok, miha.

Kaniohmi foka kakọ, Lady, ofi nafehna, ilap vt vlọssi afvmmi tuklo keyuk mvt tuchina ka̲ ant ibachvffat vtta tokạ akostininchit anta-li tokvt ak-ikhano, na, si-anukfọkah moma kvt ofu̲sik im-a̲sha tokọ isht washoha-li beka tok kia nana kaniohmi họ momat ont iksho taha tokạ ak-ikhano. Nitak aiyukali imofu̲sik mah atakla anta-li oklah ont kaniat taha yoba mah ofishki mvt si-apiesachi toba im-anukfila tok, chechuk.

Tikba Lady ishtanoa, sinti nana kaniohmi tok hikiat miti ka, ilitahina
okmvt il-itifalvmmi ahinla keyu ketok. Pih "itilhiolit" washoha hosh hvshi
kanvlli lawa e-tahli tok. Okfa patasvchi anoti kowi anuka balilit e-lhipulli
tok, micha bokushi aiawashohat oka anuka nvni e-lhioli mikmvt aiyoka-
chit e-pisa beka tok. Hvshi lawa ka nachipunta palhki hosh lhioli ayak ma
pih pisa hosh aya-li beka tok.

Hvshi 1933 fokali mah, Oklahumma yakni, okmahlika hvshi akochaka
pilla, amafo anoti sapokni ya iyakni pit e-wiha tok. Iyakni—imosapa—yvt
naksika pilla talaia toko. vlhtipo anoti chishakko nutaka il-aiasha tok. Si-
vlla moma ka hvshi elapako aiisht ilayukpa kvt moma am-ishaiali fehna
hosh vtta-li tok; kia nitak achvffa ma Lady vt abekat tasembo cha wohat
hotopat kania kia sabatakla hikiat kana't sa-bilikat vlachi ka im-issahekeyu
tok. Aki vt ant sa'shachitok ako kopoli naha mvt iakaiyat iti anoti vlhtipo
chukbikachit ont hilechih mvt, maki hikiat folohta mvt hinushi nvnih
anuka okmahli pilla bachaya imma pit balilit ia tok. Chikossi ititakla ka
pisa-li, abohli pit folotat chukoat kania tok.

Hvshi itikba kash, yakni hopaki kanihmi ho ont fallamat chuka vla
tok kia chuka ilvppano ik'lo ketok. Abeka kash yoshoblichi keyu mvt
chuka ilvppato ichuka keyu im-anukfila tok, ah chishba.

Hvshi kanohmi vttat sa-himmitat taha ako Hvshki vt chuka apanta
kowi lawa keyu vtta kvt, ofi pisa ka Lady holba hosh, hochafot chunnat
ilbvsha kania hosh imokhisa ont haiaka tok, miha. Ofi ishki ya ipetat
haknip lhakofichit tahli tok, achi.

Lady vt owatta impunna alhi beka atok. Yohmi ka Hochafo Chito
fokali ka hakshup hishi asha okla kanchi kakosh hattak lawa kvt imaimpa
ilhpak isht atahli beka tok. Chuka apanta yvt kana hosh impushnayo
atok mvt tvli holisso pokkoli atahli mvt falammint ishahinla miha tok.
Achukachvffa yvt tvli holisso mak foka ponaklo ka lauechahekeyu mvt ofi
ma ont ik-hoyo ketok.

Nan amahoba kvt Hvshki hvt am-anukfila nukhummachit isht
sa'lbvsha hinla ka ikbano mvt ofi kanima anta ka ik-amanolo ho hvshi
kanohmi vttat si-asvnochit mahaya kako okla am-anoli tok.

Hvshi kanohmi antia taha mako sapokni anoti amafo pisat aya-lik ma
chuka apanta iwanuta ofusik hishi lhafa kvt Lady chohmi hosh aiasha ho
pisa-lik mvt Lady, ofi nafehna tok ma, oklah si-anukfachi beka tok.

Anoa ilvppvt alhi, Henry Willis

I was told that Lady was left at the house by former tenants. We
moved into the house the latter part of the summer.

A year or so before, my aunt and uncle had left for Mississippi; Lady was taken along leashed under the wagon bed with a rope. Somewhere in the state of Arkansas she gnawed the rope in two and wandered across a distant part of Arkansas, crossing the Arkansas River and the greater part of Oklahoma to return home. A short piece of the rope was still around her neck as she happily trotted into the yard.

I don't recollect when Lady, the remarkable mongrel, came into the life of this two- or three-year-old boy. I only remember she had pups and I played with them but I never knew what happened to them. Perhaps my being around the pups each day until they were no longer there was the reason the mother dog became protective of me.

After the snake incident in the earlier story of Lady, we became inseparable chums. We spent many hours just playing "chase." We ran through the meadows and the woods and played down in the creek, chasing and trying to catch the fish in the water. I just watched when she was in fast pursuit of small critters.

Around 1933, we had moved to my aunt and uncle's farm in an isolated area, in the southeastern part of Oklahoma. We lived in a tent and under an arbor: it was the most joyous time of my life, until the day Lady became sick and crazy. She howled in pain but would not leave my side or let anyone near me. My dad tried to come and get me but the dog snapped at him and cornered him between a tree and the tent; she then suddenly turned and ran south along the trail toward the wooded hills. I saw her only a moment as she turned into the underbrush.

She never returned home, although she had returned from a long trip across the state years before. Perhaps she didn't consider this place to be her home or the sickness affected her sense of direction.

It was years later in my teens when my mother told me that a neighbor who lived a few miles away said a dog fitting the description of Lady came to his door tired and hungry. She was fed and restored back to health.

Lady was a very skillful hunter of game, and selling game pelts was one way to bring bread to many people's tables during the years of the Depression. The neighbor asked for ten dollars for the return of Lady back to her rightful owner. Unfortunately, my family could not afford this amount.

I suppose it was because my mother knew the mental agony I would go through that they did not tell me where the dog was until later in life.

As years passed and when I went to visit my aunt and uncle, I would see puppies with the marking of Lady in the neighbor's yard, which reminded me very much of Lady, the Remarkable Dog.

Henry Willis

Malvina Lavina Tubby Willis, the author's mother, was born in 1896 and died in 1972. In this photo, taken about 1945, she is standing on the back porch of her home in Stratford, Oklahoma. Her garden can be seen in the background. *From the author's collection.*

Anumpa *vlhpesa*: Compound Tenses

Tenses in Choctaw

We have learned that Choctaw tenses don't match perfectly with those in English. We often use the present tense in English to mark events in the future (for example, "My mother is coming this evening.") and past tense to mark things that have happened only a fraction of a second earlier ("Did you see that lightning flash?"). Other languages have their own ways of dividing up time. We have seen that in Choctaw we always use the future tense for events that have not yet come about, and we use the same present tense marker for events that are occurring at the moment and for events that have just occurred.

In Choctaw, aspect is just as important as tense in describing time. If we mark a verb with the stative or iterative aspect, it gives the sense of something occurring in some condition over a period of time, either in the present or the past. Often, that aspect is more important to the meaning than the moment in time in which it occurred.

English does not have a formal aspect system, as we know. Instead, English uses adverbs, idioms, and verbs that have their aspect "built in," such as *wear* and *own*. Additionally, English uses its set of compound tenses to create a tense and aspect system. If we say, "We eat peaches," we mean we eat them *habitually*, which is one of the aspects. If we say, "We have eaten peaches," we mean that beginning at some moment in the past and continuing up until this moment, there was a time or times when we ate peaches. This is also one of the aspects.

The Time Line: The Speaker's Perspective on Events Completed in the Past

One of the most complicated tasks in human communication is to discuss events in the past from varying points of view. Consider a simple event: The train arrived. A speaker must not only communicate the fact that the train arrived; he or she must also give some time frame for both the arrival of the train and the speech event itself. In effect, we nest two or more time frames, one inside another.

Notice the difference in meaning among the following statements. In each case, the speech event is in one time frame, and the train's arrival in another.

1. I see that the train arrived.

   This speech event is a conversational remark in the present, "I see that . . .," and the train arrival is some moment in the past.

2. When Fred reached the station, he saw that the train had arrived.

   In example 2., the speech event is perhaps a story, in some period of time in the past. There are two time frames inside this event: that in "Fred reached the station" and that in "the train had arrived." One occurs in the past *after* the other.

3. On Christmas Day, 1920, my grandfather realized the train was going to arrive.

   In example 3., the speech event is an anecdote describing a moment in the past. Inside this time frame there are two other points of time: the grandfather thinking a thought and the train arriving, the latter of which had not yet happened at the time of the thought but happened historically. This speech event describes the time frame of "future in the past."

4. This train has arrived on time since it began to run.

   In example 4., the speech event is not grounded in any strong time frame, but we assume it is the present. There is a past time point, the time when the train began to run, and a series of train arrivals that began in the past and continue to the present.

In Choctaw we manipulate three grammatical concepts—tense, aspect, and mood—to depict events and states in time frames.

"Past in the Past": *Tuk* and *tok*

We have been using the past markers in a simple fashion: *tuk* is a past marker, and *tok* is a distant past marker. We also use *tok* for narration, as in storytelling. The relationship between these markers is somewhat more complicated. We may use the past tenses together to order past events.

Notice the difference in examples a. and b. below:

a. Peni yvt ia tok<u>o</u> vla tuk.
   When he arrived, the train had left.

b. ᵾlah ma̲ peni yᵾt ia tuk.
The train left when he arrived.

In example a., we have both *tok* and *tuk*. Notice that *tok* is used to refer to an event that had already been completed at the time of another past event.

In example b., the sense is that the train left at the time the man arrived. Notice the sense of completion in the past denoted with *tok*, which is effectively translated in many cases with the English past perfect tense, *had* (Verb)-*ed*.

In Choctaw we take advantage of aspect markers to give the sense of something having gone on for a time in the past and having been completed. Notice the difference in the effects of the following examples, produced by the use of tense markers, aspect markers, and mood markers:

a. Toksaha̲li na afᵾmmi achᵾffa.
She has been working for a year [and she's still working].

Here we have the iterative aspect and present tense to give the sense of something having gone on over time and continuing.

b. Afᵾmmi achᵾffa ho̲ toksaha̲li tuk.
She worked for a year [and then she stopped].

Here the iterative aspect marker shows that she worked repeatedly and habitually over a period of time. The *tuk* tense marker indicates that this action was in the past.

c. Toksaha̲li na afᵾmmi achᵾffa tok.
She had worked for a year [at some time completed in the past and not connected to now].

In example c., again the iterative aspect marker shows that she worked repeatedly, but the *tok* tense marker indicates that this happened at some remove from other events or from now.

d. E-toksaha̲li tok kia himakano e-toksalahekeyu.
We had been working, but now we won't be working. *Or* We used to work . . .

In example d., the iterative aspect marker shows ongoing, repeated action that is complete. We may use the English expression *used to* to capture the relationship between the iterative aspect marker and *tok*. The negative mood marker *ahekeyu* indicates that this action will not begin again in the future.

The English present perfect and past perfect tenses can be used effectively to translate many Choctaw sentences.

> a. ʋllanakni ont pisa tuk.
> He's gone to see the boy.
> b. ʋllanakni pisahe atok.
> He has seen the boy.

In example b., the mood marker *ahe* emphasizes the affirmative, and the past tense marker in the form of *atok* emphasizes completion of an ongoing event or state.

Adverbs may be used effectively to enhance the sense of time:

> a. ʋllanakni ano tikbali ish-pisa tuk-o?
> Have you seen the boy before?
> b. Nittak hullo chito yash ʋllanakni pisa-li tok.
> Last Christmas I had seen the boy.
> c. Si-ʋllah momah mʋt kowa awashohowa-li chatok.
> When I was still a child, I used to play in the woods.

Past Tense in Narration

Another situation that requires both *tuk* and *tok* is the use of the recent past tense inside a story. In this case, the story is being told using the *tok* tense marker, but something happens, often as a part of a conversation, that is in the recent past with respect to the story.

> a. "Atoko yʋmma binili na alhchihba tuk, achi tok" (from chapter 9).
> So, he said he was sitting there for a little while.
> b. "'Pokni, chanʋlli apolusli lapalike tohbi himona pih himo ish-chompa tuk keyoh-o?' im-achi-li tok" (from chapter 6).
> "Auntie, didn't you just buy whitewall tires?" I said.

In these examples, the story is told in the narrative past (*achi tok* 'he said'), but what was said is marked with *tuk*.

Anumpa

Nouns

asvno	[a-sv́-no]	adult
vlhtipo	[vlh-tí-pu]	tent
bachaya	[bv-chá-yv]	course; line; row
chishakko	[chi-shák-ku]	arbor
chukbika	[chuk-bí-kv]	corner
chuka pota	[chu-kv pu-tv]	tenant
hoshotika	[ho-shó̱-ti-ka]	porch
ikonla	[i-kó̱-lv]	neck; throat
ilitahinna	[il-i-tá-hin-nv]	companion; chum
impushnayo	[i̱-push-ná-yu]	master or owner of an animal
ititakla	[i-ti̱-ták-lv]	a while; a moment
okfa patasvchi	[ok-fv pv-tá-sv-chi]	meadow; bottom land; plain
ponola	[pu-nó-lv]	cotton
ponolakvllopvna; ponolakvllo shvna	[pu-nó-lu-kl-lu-pv́-nv]; [pu-nó-lu-kvl-lu-shv́-nv]	rope
tvli holisso	[tv-li ho-lís-so]	dollar; paper money

Verbs

akostinichi	[a-kos-ti-ni̱ -chi]	recollect; have knowledge of
asvno	[a-sv-nu]	grow up
asvnochi	[a-sv-no-chi]	make an adult; cause to grow up
chukbikachi	[chuk-bí-kv-chi]	corner something
fohka	[foh-kv]	be inside
fullokachi	[ful-ló-kv-chi]	wander
ilaiyukpa	[i-lai-yuk-pv]	enjoy oneself
ishkanapa, ishkanvpa	[ish-kv-ná-pv]	happen accidentally (Gp. 2)
itakkoluffi	[i-tak-ko-luf-fi]	gnaw in two; bite into two pieces

itifilvmmi	[i-ti-fi-lvm-mi]	separate one from another
nukhvmmachi	[nuk-hvm-mi-chi]	cause pain
yoshoblichi	[yu-shó-bli-chi]	deceive; lead astray

Adjectives

lhafa	[lha-fv]	marked
naksika	[nak-sí-kv]	solitary

Adverbs

chishba	[chish-ba]	perhaps
chechuk	[ché-chuk]	perhaps; possibly
ilauet	[i-lau-et]	along with (one)
ititakla	[i-ti-tak-lv]	between
ititakla	[i-ti-tak-lv]	while; since
mihmakinli	[mih-ma-ki-li]	immediately; as soon as
maki	[ma-kí]	short form of *mihmakinli*
yoba	[yo-ba]	perhaps; maybe

Idioms

Hochafo Chito	[ho-cha-fu-chí-tu]	the Great Depression
ilauet ishtia	[i-lau-et-isht-i-v]	take along with oneself
im-issahekeyu	[im-is-sa-hé-ke-yu]	would not allow or let (someone)
okamahlika hvshi akuchaka ititakla		southeastern (literally "between the south and the east")

ANUMPA ANUKFILLI: *Issa*

This word has a great many meanings, some of which have taken on nuances that are far away from its basic meaning. *Issa* means 'quit', but it has many related synonyms: it can also mean 'release', 'abandon', or 'yield.' In its causative form, *issachi*, it means 'arrest' but also 'discharge'. When it is used with a recipient person marker, its meaning is 'promise', 'offer', 'permit', or 'let'.

a. ". . . Kana't sa-bilik̲at ꝟlachi̲ ka̲ im-issahekeyu tok."
   She wouldn't let anyone come near me.
b. ". . . Polk ato i̲kana achukma yokmꝟt nanishtꝟtta apesachi̲ ka̲ im-
   issa atok" (from chapter 7).
   Polk was easygoing, and he let her oversee the business.

Aꝟchi

Chi-anukfo̲kah-o̲?

Select three paragraphs from Mr. Willis's Choctaw story and translate
to English again, using different phrases. Note the places where you have
many choices about vocabulary and phrasing.

Anumpa ꝟlhpesa

Using tense, aspect, and mood markers, give a good Choctaw translation
for the following sentences. There is more than one correct way to do so.

1. We used to visit my uncle in Arkansas, but now we don't (visit
   him).
2. When I arrived at the school, I saw that the teacher had become
   sick.
3. It seems that the old man has been singing for a week.
4. It seemed that the young woman had been singing for an hour.
5. "Did you buy any bacon?" I asked him.
6. My relatives had never seen snow.
7. Last summer our family moved to Bokushi.
8. After we had moved to Bokushi my father sold his store.
9. He had been working in Talihina.
10. He said that he was going to quit.

Holissochi

Write a memoir describing some situation or event in the past. Be
precise in your use of tense markers.

Glossary of Terms

AFFECTED. A noun or pronoun that is in a state or condition. Marked as Group 2.

AGENT. A noun or pronoun that performs an action. Marked as Group 1.

COMPLEX PREDICATE. Two or more predicates—verbs, adjectives, or adverbs—that are used together to make a complex meaning.

COMPOUNDS. A word made up of two or more other words.

COMPOUND TENSE. A tense that includes more than one time frame or is made of both tense and aspect.

CONDITIONAL. The notion of one event being dependent on the occurrence of another.

CONTRAST. Picking out a thing or event as being distinct from others.

DEFINITENESS. The distinctions made in whether something is specific, generic, newly introduced, part of another group, referred to previously, or in contrast to something else.

DIRECTIONAL PARTICLE. Grammatical words that show whether something is taking place away from or toward the speaker.

DISCOURSE MARKERS. Special words that are used to show the speaker's attitude in conversation or to invite the listener's response.

DISJUNCTION. The sense of *or*: picking out two or more things or states of affairs that cannot be true at the same time.

EMPHATIC PARTICLE. Grammatical particle that is used to give special emphasis, positive or negative, to expressions.

FOCUS. The grammatical particles that place the listener's attention on a particular thing or event.

GRADATION. The sense of *more* and *less*.

HORTATIVE MOOD. The grammatical marking of the speaker's urging that something happen.

IDIOM. An expression that cannot be translated literally.

IMPERATIVE MOOD. The grammatical marking of the speaker's commands to others.

INDICATIVE MOOD. The grammatical marking of sentences that express simple states of affairs and questions.

MOOD. A set of verbal forms used to express the speaker's attitude toward factuality or likelihood. Moods include the indicative, subjunctive, imperative, hortative, optative, emphatic, and potential.

OPTATIVE MOOD. The grammatical marking of the speaker's expression of wishes and desires.

POSSESSIVE PREDICATE. Possession marked in the predicate rather than in a demonstrative: e.g., *mine* rather than *my*.

POTENTIAL MOOD. The grammatical marking of states of affairs that are possible but not actual.

PREDICATE. The part of a sentence that expresses what the subject does or what state the subject is in. Generally, these are verbs and adjectives.

RECIPIENT. The noun or pronoun that receives or benefits from an action. Marked as Group 3.

RECIPROCAL MARKER. The Choctaw pronoun form that marks the equivalent of the English *each other.*

REFLEXIVE MARKER. The Choctaw pronoun form that marks the equivalent of the English *oneself.*

SUBJUNCTIVE MOOD. The grammatical marking of states that are not real or are in the future.

SUPERLATIVE. The marking of adjectives to express an extreme or ultimate degree.

Choctaw-English Glossary

The order of alphabetization in Choctaw is: *v*, a, a̱, b, ch, e, f, h, i, i̱, k, l, lh, o, o̱, p, s, t, u, w, y. Pronunciation guides are not given for phrases made up of known words. Phrasal idioms appear in the Anumpa section in each chapter.

v

vbanvblichi [*v*-b*v*-n*v*b-li-chi]: put over; cause to go over
vbanvblichit pilla: throw over
vbanapoli [*v*-b*v*-na-pu-li]: jump over; pass over
vlla holissopisa shali [*v*l-l*v* ho-lis-so-pi-s*v* shá-li]: school bus
vlhpesat pisa: respect
vlhto [*v*lh-tu]: stand in; be in (plural)
vlhtipo [*v*lh-tí-pu]: tent
vmmona [*v́*m-mo-n*v*]: first
vshwanchi [*v*sh-wa̱-chi]: be engaged; be going on

a

abeka aiasha chukka [*v*-be-k*v*-áy-a-sh*v*-chúk-k*v*]: hospital
abihli [a-bih-li]: put on or insert plural things
abilia [a-bi-li-*v*]: always
aboha aialhtoka [a-bo-h*v* ai-*v*lh-tó-k*v*]: office
achakvli [a-cha-k*v*-li]: add to; unite
achaka [a-cha-k*v*]: be added to; united (Gp. 2)

141

afohommi [a-fo-hum-mi]: put on a rim
afolota [a-fo-ló-tv]: turnaround
ahvmmichi [a-hvm-mi-chi]: anoint or rub another person
ahalaia [a-ha-lai-yv]: be concerned about
ahinna [a-hin-nv]: care for or accompany someone
aholisso apisa [a-ho-lis-so a-pí-sv]: school building
aivlhi [ai-v-lhi]: end
aivlhichi [ai-v-lhi-chi]: terminate; bring to an end
aivlhpa [ai-vlh-pv]: be born somewhere (Gp. 2)
aiatokko [ai-v-tok-ku]: shelter
aialhi ka [áy-a-lhi-ka]: sure enough; of course
aiiklanachi [ai-ik-lv-na-chi]: put in the middle of
aiisht ahollo [ay-isht-v-hól-lu]: miracle
aiithana vlhi [ai-i-ta-nv v-lhi]: memoir
aiitibi [ay-i-tí-bi]: battle; fight
akachanlichi [a-kv-chá-li-chi]: plus; in addition
akkaya [ak-ka-yv]: go on foot
akkia [ák-ki-v]: along with; also; too
akkoa, akkowa [ák-ko-wv]: get down; descend; dismount
akmo [ak-mu]: harden; congeal; stiffen; hardened; congealed
akohcha [a-koh-chv]: come out of; escape
akostininchi [v-kos-ti-ni-chi]: find out; discover; have knowledge of
alaka [a-lv-ka]: edge; border
alaui [a-lau-i]: equal; adequate
alauichi [v-lau-i-chi]: do equally
albo [ál-bu]: forest undergrowth
alhowvlit yukpachi [a-lho-wv-lit yuk-pa-chi]: entertain; joke
alhoffi [a-lhof-fi]: skin; strip
alotali [a-lo-tv-li]: pack; load
anumpulit chokvsh hotopali: insult
apaknakachi [a-pak-ná-kv-chi]: get on top of something; go overhead
apata [v-pa-tv]: on the side of; along the side of
apitta [a-pit-tv]: put plural things into something
apolusli [a-po-lús-li]: tire; casing
ashachi [a-sha-chi]: store; put away
ashila [a-shí-lv]: dry spot among wet ones
atakohchi [a-ta-kóh-chi]: clothesline
atia [á-ti-yv]: way; passage

b
bᴠsht tᴠbli [bᴠsht tᴠb-li]: amputate; cut off
bᴠska [bᴠs-kᴠ]: gamble; bet
bachaya [bᴠ-chá-yᴠ]: course; line; row
bachoha [bᴠ-cho-hᴠ]: lie in rows or lanes (pl. of *bachaya*)
bakli [bak-li]: split something into large pieces
bicheli [bi-che-li]: draw liquid from a container

ch
chᴠffichi [chᴠf-fi-chi]: send off
chᴠfichi [chᴠ-fí-chi]: driver
chahikli [cha-hik-li]: limp (walk)
chatok, chatuk [cha-tok]: ever in the past
chatosh [cha-tush]: ever habitually
chatosh ba [cha-tush ba]: never habitually
chechuk [ché-chuk]: perhaps; possibly
chishakko [chi-shák-ku]: arbor
chishba [chish-ba]: perhaps
chokᴠsh chaha: high-spirited
chuka pota [chu-kᴠ pu-tᴠ]: tenant
chukbika [chuk-bí-kᴠ]: corner
chukbikachi [chuk-bí-kᴠ-chi]: corner something
chukka ᴠpishia [chu-kᴠ ᴠ-pi-shé-ᴠ]: porch
chukka asha [chuk-ká-shᴠ]: family
chukka haiaka [chuk-kᴠ hái-ya-kᴠ]: country home
chukka itabana [chuk-kᴠ i-tᴠ-bá-nᴠ]: log house
chukka lokoli [chuk-kᴠ lu-kó-li]: neighborhood

f
faloha [fᴠ-ló-hᴠ]: long (plural)
filemoa [fi-le-mo-ᴠ]: turn this way and that
filemoat pit pisa: look around
fochik [fú-chik]: star (variant of *fichik*)
fohka [foh-kᴠ]: be inside

h
hᴠshi kanᴠlli [hᴠ-shi ka-nᴠl-li]: hour
haiyokpulo okchaki [hai-yok-pu-lo ok-chá-ki]: salad; greens

hal*v*lli [ha-l*v*l-li]: draw together; marry
himmaka pilla [him-ma-ka pil-l*v*]: from now on
himonasi [hi-mó-n*v*-si]: minute
hina ikp*v*tho [hi-n*v* ik-p*v*t-ho]: lane (of road)
hina p*v*tha [hi-n*v* p*v*t-h*v*]: paved road; highway
hiya [he-ya]: perhaps
Hochafo Chito [ho-cha-fu-chí-tu]: the Great Depression
hochukma [ho-chúk-m*v*]: good (plural)
hofanti [ho-f<u>a</u>-ti]: grow up (Gp. 2)
holba toba [hol-b*v* tó-b*v*]: picture
holisso itibapishi [ho-lis-su i-ti-bá-pi-shi]: schoolmate
hosh<u>o</u>tika [ho-sh<u>ó</u>-ti-ka]: porch

i
i*v*lli [i-*v*l-li]: thing of value; money
i*v*lli isht ayopomo: waste money on
ibataklat <u>a</u>ya: hang around with someone
ibbak afabik imma [ib-bak a-fa-bik ím-m*v*]: left hand
ibbak fohka [ib-bak fóh-k*v*]: gloves
ichapa [i-chá-p*v*]: team
ikonla [i-k<u>ó</u>-l*v*]: neck; throat
ilap ahni lhamko: strong-willed
ilap<u>i</u>t ikbi: make by oneself; homemade
ilatomba [i-la-t<u>o</u>-b*v*]: save
ilauet [i-lau-et]: along with (one)
ilauet ishtia [i-lau-et-isht-i-*v*]: take along with oneself
im-alheka [im-*v*-lhe-k*v*]: be painful to (Gp. 3)
imalheka [i-ma-lhé-k*v*]: unfortunate
imalhekahekeyu [i-ma-lhe-k*v*-hé-ki-yu]: safe ('not unsafe')
imalhekahinla [i-ma-lhe-k*v*-hi-l*v*]: unsafe
im-isht *v*tta [im-isht *v*t-t*v*]: be in service; occupied (Gp. 3)
imisht asha [i-misht á-sh*v*]: the (military) service
imissa [im-is-s*v*]: to let; permit; offer (recipient object)
imom*v*chi [i-mó-m*v*-chi]: old; experienced
imoma [i-mo-m*v*]: natural
imomaka [i-mó-m*v*-ka]: experience
imomika fochik: guiding star
impushnayo [<u>i</u>-push-ná-yu]: master or owner of an animal

im-pussi [i-pus-si]: kiss (recipient object)
ipo [e-pu]: sister-in-law
ippochihoyo [ip-po-chi-hó-yu]: sister-in-law; mother-in-law
ishkanapa, ishkanʋpa [ish-kʋ-ná-pʋ]: happen accidentally; become
     bewitched (Gp. 2)
ishtaiopi [isht-ái-yo-pi]: last
isht bakli tiwa [isht bak-li tí-wʋ]: breach block
ishtochi [isht-ó-chi]: bucket
isht onnuchi: take by lawful force
ishttoksali [isht-tók-sʋ-li]: machine; tool
iskʋlli apota [is-kʋl-li a-pó-tʋ]: bank (financial)
issito holba [is-si-to-hól-bʋ]: cucumber
issitushi [is-si-tú-shi]: squash
itabʋni [i-ta-bʋ-ni]: put together by fitting pieces to another
itabana [i-ta-ba-nʋ]: be fit into each other, as logs in a log house
itahinna [i-tá-hi-nʋ]: companion; chum
itaichapa, itachapa [i-ta-i-cha-pʋ]: matched
itayokoma [i-ta-yu-ko-mʋ]: scramble out; mixed up
itihalʋlli [i-ti ha-lʋl-li]: get married
iti kʋfi [i-ti kʋ-fi]: sassafras tree
itilaui [i-te-lau-i]: matched
itilauichi [i-ti-lau-i-chi]: do the same as each other
iti lumbo [i-ti ló-bu]: log
iti nakshish [i-ti nák-shish]: tree limb; bush
itifilʋmmi [i-ti-fi-lʋm-mi]: separate one from another
ititakla [i-ti-ták-lʋ]: while; since; a while; a moment
itombi [i-tó-bi]: box; square container
itontalaha [i-to-tʋ-lá-ha]: story; floor (of building)
iyasha [i-yá-shʋ]: iron cauldron
iyup [í-yup]: son-in-law

i
i-hiohli [i-hi-oh-li]: have plural things (Gp. 3)
ikana achukma: easy-going
ipota [i-pu-tʋ]: lend to someone (recipient object)

k
kʋna; kana moma: everybody
kana kia: someone; anyone

kanali [ka-na-li]: move
kanihmi [ka-níh-mi]: healing; convalescing
kanima kashinli [kv-ni-mv ka-shi̠-li]: sometime
kanomona; kanohmona [ka-no-mó-nv]: several; many
kapali [ka-pá-li]: bridle bit
kapali isht talakchi [ka-pa-li isht ta-lák-chi]: reins
kinakli [ki-nak-li]: move sporadically; stumble
kisha [ké-shv]: not yet; not even yet
kowi [kó-wi]: mile
kulli [kúl-li]: spring (of water); well

l
lvpa [lv-pv]: blind
lapalika [lv-pa-li-ka]: the side
laue, lauwi [lau-e]: equal
litoli [li-to-li]: crush; smash
lobolichi [lu-bo-li-chi]: boil something
lobochi [lo-bo̠-chi]: boiled
lokoli, lukoli [lu-ko-li]: cluster or group together
lukfi nuna [luk-fi nú-nv]: brick

lh
lhilahli [lhi-láh-li]: mangled; torn in many places
lhitohkachi [lhi-toh-kv-chi]: rewind; roll down

m
mvlahtushi [mv-láh-tu-shi]: electricity
mvlha [mv-lhv]: tin pan
mvlhi [mv-lhi]: doubtless; truly
maiya [mai-yv]: to go forward; to pass
mak fokali ma [mak fo-ka-li ma]: at about that time
makashinli [ma-kv-shi̠-li]: the same as
mihmvt [mih-mvt]: and then; and (same subject)
mihma [mih-ma]: and then; and
mihmakinli [mih-ma-ki̠-li]: immediately; as soon as; at the same time or
    place
mika̠ [mi-ka̠]: short form of *mihmakinli*
mishema [mi-she-mv]: farther; farther off

n

nachⱴfichi'sh ạya: go driving
nachefa [na-che-fⱴ]: do the wash; launder
naki lumbo [na-ki lum-bu]: bullet
naknossi [nak-nos-si]: little boy
naksika [nak-sí-kⱴ]: solitary
nana hokano [na-na-hó-kⱴ-no]: something; some thing or another
nana họ kaniohmi: whatever one does
nana kạ: whatever; something like that
nanalhto [na-nálh-tu]: container; bucket
nanimatahli [na-ni-ma-táh-li]: hospitality; service
nanishtⱴtta [na-nisht-ⱴt-tⱴ]: business
nanishthalⱴlli [nan-isht-hⱴ-lⱴ́l-li]: tractor
nanishtịkana [na-nisht-i-kánⱴ]: peace
nashali [na-shá-li]: car
nihi lⱴwa [ni-hi lⱴ-wⱴ]: tomato (and other seeded fruits)
nipi patoa [ni-pi pⱴ-tó-ⱴ]: ground meat
nittak hollo [nit-tak hól-lu]: week
nukhⱴmmichi [nuk-hⱴm-mi-chi]: cause pain
nukhạklot anoli: apologize
nutakachi [nu-tá-kⱴ-chi]: put beneath; place under

o

ochak [ó-chⱴk]: cantaloupe
ochi [o-chi]: draw water with a bucket from a well
oka abicheli [o-kⱴ a-bi-ché-li]: running water
oka alaka [o-kⱴ a-lⱴ-ka]: shore
okakania [o-kⱴ-kⱴ-ni-yⱴ]: sink; drown; become mired
okamahlika hⱴshi akuchaka ititakla: southeastern
Oka Peni Ishtasha [o-kⱴ pe-ni isht-á-shⱴ]: the navy
okchilhont pisa [ok-chi-lhọt pi-sⱴ]: stare at
okfa patasⱴchi [ok-fⱴ pⱴ-tá-sⱴ-chi]: meadow; bottom land; plain
olⱴlli [o-lⱴl-li]: laugh at; mock
olhkⱴchi, ulhkⱴchi [ulh-ko-chi]: canned; soaked; steeped
olhti [ólh-ti]: government
ome atokia: well; however; and so
omikato [o-mí-ka-to]: expression of surprise: well! my goodness!
ompohomo, umpohomo [ọ-pu-ho-mu]: cover; bury; covered with; buried

onochi [o-nu-chi]: blame
opia [o-pi-yv]: become evening; get dark
opiaka [o-pí-yv-ka]: evening

o̲

o̲kof [ó̲-kuf]: persimmon
o̲weli [o̲-we-li]: aim a gun at

p
pvchi yoshoba [pv-chi yo-shó-bv]: dove
pvla vlhtaha [pv-lv vlh-tá-ha]: electric lights
pvla mvlahtushi shapoa: lamp
pvlhkichi [pvlh-ki-chi]: cause to be fast; drive fast
pvtha [pvt-hv]: wide
pa̲shpoa [pá̲sh-pu-v]: broomcorn
peni isht vtta [pe-ni isht vt-tv]: sailor
pilla [pil-lv]: from; off in distant space or time
poa alhpoa [po-v alh-pó-v]: pet
polohlichi [pu-loh-li-chi]: cause to spark
ponola [pu-nó-lv]: cotton
ponolakvllopvna [pu-nó-lu-kvl-lu-pv́-nv]: rope
ponolakvllo shvna [pu-nó-lu-kvl-lu-shv́-nv]: rope

s
salahachi [sv-la-ha-chi]: slow down
shahli [shah-li]: excessively
shakapa [shv-ká-pv]: turmoil; uproar
shanaioa [shv-nai-o-wv]: weave; swerve
shapulechi [sha-pu-le-chi]: work in a harness
shohbi [shoh-bi]: all day; the day up until the evening
shoyohbi [shó-yoh-bi]: (intensive) all day long; all the live-long day
shukshi [shúk-shi]: watermelon

t
tvkohlit maya [tv-koh-lit ma-yv]: be somewhere sporadically (pl.)
tvli pvtha [tv-li pvt-hv]: pavement
tvli pvtha anowa [tv-li pvt-hv a-nó-wv]: paved walkway
tabokoli, tabokuli [tv-bó-ku-li]: be noon
tabokoli ontia [tv-bó-ku-li o̲t-ia]: afternoon
takali [ta-ká-li]: connected

takali [tv-ka-li]: be in a position; hang; hung up; stuck;
takalichi [tv-ká-li-chi]: hang or suspend something
takohlichi [ta-koh-li-chi]: hang up plural things
takohmaya [ta-koh-má-yv]: clothesline
talaia [tv-lai-yv]: be set; be placed somewhere
talali [tv-la-li]: set in place; put somewhere
taloha [ta-lo-hv]: be set or placed somewhere (plural things)
talohli [ta-loh-li]: set plural things in place
talohmaya [ta-loh-ma-yv]: stand around
takla [tak-lv]: during; while
tikba [tík-bv]: ancestors; first; before
tikba hiket ishtia: take charge
tilikpi [ti-lik-pi]: shield
tomba [to-bv]: very

u
ulbal [ul-bal]: the back; the rear; behind; in the rear
ulbal abohli [ul-bal-a-bóh-li]: backwoods

w
wakeli [wa-ke-li]: lift; raise up
walakshi [wv-lák-shi]: Choctaw dumplings
walhvllichi [wa-lhvl-li-chi]: cause to boil
weheli; weli [we-he-li]: take out plural things

y
yvmmaki [yvm-mv-kí]: so; thus
yvmmak kia [yvm-mak ki-v]: likewise, also
yvmmimma [yvm-mim-mv]: that way
yakni fullota [yak-ni fúl-lo-tv]: region; area
yakni holitushi [yak-ni ho-li-tú-shi]: lot; pen
Yakni Moma Tvnvp Atukla: World War II
yakni talhkachi [yakni tvlh-ka-chi]: islands
yakni tashaya [yak-ni tv-shá-yv]: island
yohmi [yoh-mi]: be so; and such
yohmi atukkia [yoh-mi-v-túk-ki-yv]: well; anyway
yohmi mvlhi kiyo kia [yoh-mi-mv-lhi-kí-yo-ki-yv]: still; of course; but of
    course
yopomo [yu-po-mu]: waste

English-Choctaw Glossary

a
add to: achakʋli [a-cha-kʋ-li]
adequate: alaui [a-lau-i]
afternoon: tabokoli ontia [tʋ-bó-ku-li o̱t-ia]
all day; the day up until the evening: shohbi [shoh-bi]
all day long: shoyohbi [shó-yoh-bi]
along with; also; too: akkia [ák-ki-ʋ]
along with (one): ilauet [i-lau-et]
always: abilia [a-bi-li-ʋ]
amputate: bʋsht tʋbli [bʋsht tʋb-li]
ancestors: tikba [tík-bʋ]
and then; and: mihma [mih-ma]
and then; and (same subject): mihmʋt [mih-mʋt]
anoint or rub another person: ahʋmmichi [a-hʋm-mi-chi]
anyone: kana kia [kʋ-nʋ ki-yʋ]
apologize: nukhaklot anoli
arbor: chishakko [chi-shák-ku]
arrest: isht onnuchi [isht ó̱n-nʋ-chi]
at about that time: mak fokali ma [mak fo-ka-li ma]

b
back; behind: ulbal [ul-bal]
backwoods: ulbal abohli [ul-bal-a-bóh-li]
bank (financial): iskʋlli apota [is-kʋl-li a-pó-tʋ]

151

battle: aiitibi [ay-i-tí-bi]
be; hang: takali [tv-ka-li]
be added to; united (Gp. 2): achaka [a-cha-kv]
be born somewhere (Gp. 2): aivlhpa [ai-vlh-pv]
be concerned about: ahalaia [a-ha-lai-yv]
be engaged; be going on: vshwanchi [vsh-wa̱-chi]
be fit into each other, as logs in a log house: itabana [i-ta-ba-nv]
be in service; be occupied (Gp. 3): im-isht vtta [im-isht vt-tv]
be inside: fohka [foh-kv]
be painful to (Gp. 3): im-alheka [im-v-lhe-kv]
be set; be placed somewhere: talaia [tv-lai-yv]
be set or placed somewhere (plural things): taloha [ta-lo-hv]
be so; and such: yohmi [yoh-mi]
be somewhere sporadically (pl.): tvkohlit maya [tv-koh-lit ma-yv]
become evening; get dark: opia [o-pi-yv]
blame: onochi [o-nu-chi]
blind: lvpa [lv-pv]
boil something: lobolichi [lu-bo-li-chi]
boiled: lobochi [lo-bo̱-chi]
box; square: itombi [i-tó̱-bi]
breach block: isht bakli tiwa [isht bak-li tí-wv]
brick: lukfi nuna [luk-fi nú-nv]
bridle bit: kapali [ka-pá-li]
broomcorn: pashpoa [pá̱sh-pu-v]
bucket: ishtochi [isht-ó-chi]
bury (a creature): hoppi, hohpi [huh-pi]
bush: iti nakshish [i-ti nák-shish]
business: nanishtvtta [na-nisht-vt-tv]

c
canned: olhkvchi, ulhkvchi [ulh-ko-chi]
cantaloupe: ochak [ó-chvk]
car: nashali [na-shá-li]
care for or accompany someone: ahinna [a-hin-nv]
cause pain: nukhvmmichi [nuk-hvm-mi-chi]
cause to be fast; drive fast: pvlhkichi [pvlh-ki-chi]
cause to boil: walhvllichi [wa-lhvl-li-chi]
cause to spark: pohlolichi [puh-lo-li-chi]
Choctaw dumplings: walakshi [wv-lák-shi]

clothesline: atakohchi [a-ta-kóh-chi]
clothesline: takohmaya [ta-koh-má-y*v*]
cluster; group together: lokoli, lukoli [lu-ko-li]
come down: akkoa [ák-k*v*-w*v*]
come out of: akohcha [a-koh-ch*v*]
companion; chum: itahinna [i-tá-hin-n*v*]
connected: takali [ta-ká-li]
container; bucket: nanalhto [na-nálh-tu]
corner: chukbika [chuk-bí-k*v*]
corner something: chukbikachi [chuk-bí-k*v*-chi]
cotton: ponola [pu-nó-l*v*]
country home: chukka haiaka [chuk-k*v* hái-ya-k*v*]
course; line; row: bachaya [b*v*-chá-y*v*]
cover; covered with: ompohomo, umpohomo [o̲-pu-ho-mu]
crush: litoli [li-to-li]
cucumber: issito holba [is-si-to-hól-b*v*]
cut off: b*v*sht t*v*bli [b*v*sht t*v*b-li]

d
descend: akkoa [ák-k*v*-w*v*]
do the wash; launder: nachefa [na-che-f*v*]
doubtless; truly: m*v*lhi [m*v*-lhi]
dove: p*v*chi yoshoba [p*v*-chi yo-shó-b*v*]
draw liquid from a container: bicheli [bi-che-li]
draw together: halvlli [ha-l*v*l-li]
draw water with a bucket from a well: ochi [o-chi]
driver: ch*v*fichi [ch*v*-fí-chi]
dry spot among the wet ones: ashi̲la [a-shí̲-l*v*]
during; while: ta̲kla [ta̲k-l*v*]

e
easygoing: i̲kana achukma [i̲-ka-n*v*-chuk-m*v*]
edge; border: alaka [a-l*v*-ka]
electric lights: p*v*la *v*lhtaha [p*v*-l*v* *v*lh-tá-ha]
electricity: m*v*lahtushi [m*v*-láh-tu-shi]
entertain; joke: alhow*v*lit yukpa̲chi [a-lho-w*v*-lit yuk-pa̲-chi]
equal: laue, lauwi [lau-e], alaui [a-lau-i]
escape: akohcha [a-koh-ch*v*]
ever (habitually): chatosh [cha-tush]

ever in the past: chatok [cha-tok]
everybody: kѵna moma [kѵ-na mo-mѵ]
excessively: shahli [shah-li]
experience: imomaka [i-mó-mѵ-ka]

f
family: chukka asha [chuk-ká-shѵ]
farther; farther off: mishema [mi-she-mѵ]
fight: aiitibi [ay-i-tí-bi]
find out; discover; have knowledge of: akostininchi [ѵ-kos-ti-ni̱-chi]
first: ѵmmona [ѵ́m-mo-nѵ]; tikba [tik-bѵ]
forest undergrowth: albo [ál-bu]
from; off in a distant space or time: pilla [pil-lѵ]
from now on: himmaka pilla [him-ma-ka pil-lѵ]

g
gamble; bet: bѵska [bѵs-kѵ]
get married: itihalѵlli [i-ti ha-lѵl-li]
get on top of something; go overhead: apaknakachi [a-pak-ná-kѵ-chi]
gloves: ibbak fohka [ib-bak fóh-kѵ]
go down; get down; dismount: akkoa, akkowa [ak-ko-ѵ]
go driving: nachѵfichi'sh a̱ya [na-chѵ-fi-chish a-yѵ]
go forward; pass: maiya [mai-yѵ]
good (plural): hochukma [ho-chúk-mѵ]
government: olhti [ólh-ti]
Great Depression: Hochafo Chito [ho-cha-fu-chí-tu]
ground meat: nipi patoa [ni-pi pѵ-tó-ѵ]
grow up (Gp. 2): hofanti [ho-fa̱-ti]
guiding star: imomika fochik

h
hang around with someone: ibataklat a̱ya [i-ba-tak-lѵt a̱-yѵ]
hang; hung up; stuck; hooked: takali [ta-ka-li]
hang or suspend something: takalichi [tѵ-ká-li-chi]
hang up plural things: takohlichi [ta-koh-li-chi]
happen accidentally; become bewitched (Gp. 2): ishkanapa; ishkanѵpa
[ish-kѵ-ná-pѵ]
harden; congeal; stiffen; hardened; congealed: akmo [ak-mu]
have plural things (Gp. 3): i̱-hiohli [i̱-hi-oh-li]

healing; convalescing: kanihmi [ka-níh-mi]
high-spirited: cho̱kv̱sh chaha [cho̱-kv̱sh chá-ha]
highway: hina pv̱tha [hi-nv̱ pv̱t-hv̱]
homemade: ilapi̱t ikbi [i-la-pi̱t íkbi]
hospital: abeka aiasha chukka [v̱-be-kv̱-áy-a-shv̱-chúk-kv̱]
hospitality; service: nanimatahli [na-ni-ma-táh-li]
hour: hv̱shi kanv̱lli [hv̱-shi ka-nv̱l-li]

i

immediately; as soon as; at the same time or place: mihmakinli
     [mih-ma-ki̱-li]
insult: anumpulit cho̱kv̱sh hotopali
iron cauldron: iyasha [i-yá-shv̱]
island: yakni tashaya [yak-ni tv̱-shá-yv̱]
islands: yakni talhkachi [yakni tv̱lh-ka-chi]

k
kiss: im-pussi [i̱-pus-si]

l
lamp: pv̱la mv̱lahtushi shapoa
lane (of road): hina ikpv̱tho [hi-nv̱ ik-pv̱t-ho]
last: ishtaiopi [isht-ái-yo-pi]
laugh at; mock: olv̱lli [o-lv̱l-li]
left hand: ibbak afabik imma [ib-bak a-fa-bik ím-mv̱]
lend to someone: i̱pota [i̱-pu-tv̱]
let; permit; offer: im-issa [im-is-sv̱]
lie in rows or lanes: bachoha [bv̱-cho-hv̱]
lift; raise up: wakeli [wa-ke-li]
likewise; also: yv̱mmak kia [yv̱m-mak ki-v̱]
limp (walk): chahikli [cha-hik-li]
log: iti lumbo [i-ti ló-bu]
log house: chukka itabana [chuk-kv̱ i-tv̱-bá-nv̱]
long (plural): faloha [fv̱-ló-hv̱]
look around: filemoat pit pisa [fi-le-mu-v̱t pit pi-sv̱]
lot; pen: yakni holitushi [yak-ni ho-li-tú-shi]

m
machine; tool: ishtto̱ksali [isht-tó̱k-sv̱-li]
make by oneself: ilapi̱t ikbi [i-la-pi̱t ik-bi]

mangled; torn in many places: lhilahli [lhi-láh-li]
marry: hal𝑣lli [ha-l𝑣l-li]
master or owner of an animal, or of a person: impushnayo [i̱-push-ná-yu]
matched: itaichapa, itachapa [i-ta-i-cha-p𝑣]; itilaui [i-te-lau-i]
meadow; bottom land: okfa patas𝑣chi [ok-f𝑣 p𝑣-tá-s𝑣-chi]
memoir: aiithana 𝑣lhi [ai-i-ta-n𝑣 𝑣-lhi]
mile: kowi [kó-wi]
military service: imisht asha [i-misht á-sh𝑣]
miracle: aiisht ahollo [ay-isht-𝑣-hól-lu]
move: kanali [ka-na-li]
move sporadically; stumble: kinakli [ki-nakli]

n
natural: imoma [i-mo-m𝑣]
navy: Oka Peni Ishtasha [o-k𝑣 pe-ni isht-á-sh𝑣]
neck; throat: ikonla [i-kó̱-l𝑣]
neighborhood: chukka lokoli [chuk-k𝑣 lu-kó-li]
never (habitually): chatoshba [cha-tush-ba]
noon: tabokoli, tabokuli [t𝑣-bó-ku-li]
not yet; not even yet: kisha [ké-sh𝑣]

o
office: aboha aialhtoka [a-bo-h𝑣 ai-𝑣lh-tó-k𝑣]
old; experienced: imom𝑣chi [i-mó-m𝑣-chi]
on the side of; along the side of: apata [𝑣-pa-t𝑣]

p
pack; load: alotali [a-lo-t𝑣-li]
part from each other: iti̱fil𝑣mmi [i-ti fi-l𝑣m-mi]
paved road: hina p𝑣tha [hi-n𝑣 p𝑣t-h𝑣]
paved walkway: t𝑣li p𝑣tha anowa [t𝑣-li p𝑣t-h𝑣 a-nó-w𝑣]
pavement: t𝑣li p𝑣tha [t𝑣-li p𝑣t-h𝑣]
peace: nanisht̲i̲kana [na-nisht-i̱-kán𝑣]
perfectly: itilaui 𝑣lhpesa [i-te-lau-i 𝑣lh-pe-s𝑣]
perhaps: chishba [chish-ba]
perhaps; possibly: chechuk [ché-chuk]
persimmon: o̱kof [ó̱-kuf]
pet: poa alhpoa [po-𝑣 alh-pó-𝑣]
picture: holba toba [hol-b𝑣 tó-b𝑣]

plain: okfa patasⱴchi [ok-fⱴ pⱴ-tá-sⱴ-chi]
plus; in addition: akachanlichi [a-kⱴ-chá̱-li-chi]
porch: chukka ⱴpishia [chu-kⱴ ⱴ-pi-shé-ⱴ]; hoshotika [ho-shó̱-ti-ka]
put beneath; place under: nutakachi [nu-tá-kⱴ-chi]
put in the middle of: aiiklanachi [ai-ik-lⱴ-na-chi]
put on a rim: afohommi [a-fo-hum-mi]
put on or insert plural things: abihli [a-bih-li]
put over; cause to go over: ⱴbanⱴblichi [ⱴ-bⱴ-nⱴb-li-chi]
put plural things into something: apitta [a-pit-tⱴ]
put together by fitting pieces to another: itabⱴni [i-ta-bⱴ-ni]

r
rear; in the rear: ulbal [ul-bal]
region; area: yakni fullota [yak-ni fúl-lo-tⱴ]
reins: kapali isht talakchi [ka-pa-li isht ta-lák-chi]
respect: ⱴlhpesat pisa
rope: ponolakⱴllo shⱴna [pu-nó-lu-kⱴl-lu-shⱴ́-nⱴ]; ponolakⱴllopⱴna
    [pu-nó-lu-kⱴl-lu-pⱴ́-nⱴ]
running water: oka abicheli [o-kⱴ a-bi-ché-li]

s
safe: imalhekahekeyu [i-ma-lhe-kⱴ-hé-ki-yu]
sailor: peni isht ⱴtta [pe-ni isht ⱴt-tⱴ]
salad; greens: haiyokpulo okchaki [hai-yok-pu-lo ok-chá̱-ki]
sassafras tree: iti kⱴfi [i-ti kⱴ-fi]
save: ilatomba [i-la-to̱-bⱴ]
school building: aholisso apisa [a-ho-lis-so a-pí-sⱴ]
school bus: ⱴlla holissopisa shali [ⱴl-lⱴ ho-lis-so-pi-sⱴ shá-li]
schoolmate: holisso itibapishi [ho-lis-su i-ti-bá-pi-shi]
scramble out; mixed up: itayokoma [i-ta-yu-ko-mⱴ]
send off: chⱴffichi [chⱴf-fi-chi]
separate one from another: itifilⱴmmi [i-ti-fi-lⱴm-mi]
set in place; put somewhere: talali [tⱴ-la-li]
set plural things in place: talohli [ta-loh-li]
several; many: kanomona, kanohmona [ka-no-mó-nⱴ]
shore: oka alaka [o-kⱴ a-lⱴ-ka]
side: lapalika [lⱴ-pa-li-ka]
sink: okakania [o-kⱴ-kⱴ-ni-yⱴ]
sister-in-law: ippochihoyo [ip-po-chi-hó-yu]; ipo [e-pu]

slow down: salahachi [sע-la-ha-chi]
smash: litoli [li-to-li]
so; thus: yעmmak̲i [yעm-mע-kí]
soaked, steeped: olhkעchi, ulhkעchi [ulh-ko-chi]
solitary: naksika [nak-sí-kע]
someone; anyone: kana kia [kע-nע ki-yע]
something; some thing or another: nana hokano [na-na-hó-kע-no]
sometime: kanima kashinli [k-ni-mעa kash i̲-li]
son-in-law: iyup [í-yup]; ippok [ip-puk]
southeastern: okamahlika hעshi akuchaka it̲itakla [okע-máh-li-ka hע-shi a-kú-chע-ka i-t̲i-tak-lע]
split something into large pieces: bakli [bak-li]
spring (of water); well: kulli [kúl-li]
squash: issitushi [is-si-tú-shi]
stand around: talohmaya [ta-loh-ma-yע]
stand in; be in, plural: עlhto [עlh-tu]
star: fochik [fú-chik] (variant of *fichik*)
stare at: okchilhont pisa [ok-chi-lh̲ot pi-sע]
still; of course; but of course: yohmi mעlhi kiyo kia [yoh-mi-mע-lhi-kí-yo-ki-yע]
store; put away: ashachi [a-sha-chi]
story; floor (of building): itontalaha [i-t̲o-tע-lá-ha]
strong-willed: ilap ahni lhamko [i-láp ah-ni lhám-ku]
sure enough; of course: aia̲lhi k̲a [áy-a̲-lhi-k̲a]
swerve: shanaioa [shע-nai-o-wע]

t
take along with oneself: ilauet ishtia [i-lau-et-isht-i-ע]
take charge: tikba hiket ishtia [tik-ba hi-két isht-i-yע]
take out plural things: weheli, weli [we-he-li]
team: ichapa [i-chá-pע]
tenant: chuka pota [chu-kע pu-tע]
tent: עlhtipo [עlh-tí-pu]
terminate; bring to an end: aiעlhichi [ai-ע-lhi-chi]
that way: yעmmimma [yעm-mim-mע]
the same as: makashinli [ma-kע-sh̲i-li]
thing of value; money: iעlli [i-עl-li]
throw over: עbanעblichit pilla
tire; casing: apolusli [a-po-lús-li]

tomato (and other seeded fruits): nihi lʋwa [ni-hi lʋ-wʋ]
tractor: nanishthalʋlli [nan-isht-hʋ-lʋ́l-li]
tree limb: iti nakshish [i-ti nák-shish]
turmoil; uproar: shakapa [shʋ-ká-pʋ]
turn this way and that: filemoa [fi-le-mo-ʋ]
turnaround: afolota [a-fo-ló-tʋ]

u
unfortunate: imalheka [i-ma-lhé-kʋ]
unite: achakʋli [a-cha-kʋ-li]
unsafe: imalhekahinla [i-ma-lhe-kʋ-hi̱-lʋ]

v
very: tomba [to̱-bʋ]

w
waste: yopomo [yu-po-mu]
waste money on: ivlli isht ayopomo [i-yʋl-li isht a-yo-po-mu]
watermelon: shukshi [shúk-shi]
way; passage: atia [á-ti-yʋ]
week: nittak hollo [nit-tak hól-lu]
well; anyway: yohmi atukkia [yoh-mi-ʋ-túk-ki-yʋ]
well; however; and so: ome atokkia [o-mé a-tok-ki-yʋ]
whatever; something like that: nana ka̱
whatever one does: nana ho̱ kaniohmi [na-nʋ ho̱ kʋ-ni-oh-mi]
while; since; a while; a moment: iti̱takla [i-ti̱-ták-lʋ]
wide: pʋtha [pʋt-hʋ]
work in a harness: shapulechi [sha-pu-le-chi]; shanaioa [shʋ-nai-o-wʋ]
World War II: Yakni Moma Tʋnʋp Atu̱kla [yak-ni mo-mʋ tʋ-nʋp a-to̱k-lʋ]

Contributors

Marcia Haag is an associate professor of linguistics at the University of Oklahoma in Norman.

Jay McAlvain is retired and lives in Seminole, Oklahoma.

Phillip Carroll Morgan is a graduate student in English and Native American literature at the University of Oklahoma.

Grayson Noley is a professor of educational leadership at the University of Oklahoma.

Bill Nowlin is retired and lives in Huntsville, Texas.

Lois McAlvain Pugh passed away in May 2007. She lived in McAlester, Oklahoma.

Eveline Battiest Steele is a Choctaw teacher in Broken Bow, Oklahoma.

Tim Tingle is a Choctaw folklorist and author living in Canyon Lake, Texas.

Henry Willis is a Choctaw teacher, researcher, and author living in Moore, Oklahoma.

Index

Milton Keynes UK
Ingram Content Group UK Ltd.
UKHW041327301024
2473UKWH00021B/88